ABA Programs for Kids with Autism
A guide for parents and caregivers

Dr. Gary Brown

Copyright © 2014 Dr. Gary Brown

All rights reserved.

ABA Programs for Kids with Autism

Based on:
APPLIED BEHAVIORAL ANALYSIS (ABA) PROGRAMS FOR KIDS WITH AUTISM OR OTHER NEUROPSYCHOLOGICAL DISORDERS: A BRIEF NON-TECHNICAL GUIDE FOR PARENTS AND OTHER CAREGIVERS

By Gary Brown, Ph.D.
Psychologist/HSP
**Children's Treatment Center for Autism
or other Childhood Developmental Disorders**
Martin, TN 38238
www.childrenstreatmentcenter4autism.com

Copyright 2001 by Gary Brown, Ph.D. All rights reserved.
Updated and edited by Bob Bradley 2012, 2014.

© 2012-2014 Dr. Brown's Apps, LLC
Updated and published in Amazon Kindle Direct Publishing 2014 by Dr. Brown's Apps, LLC, Martin, Tennessee

Updated and published in CreateSpace Publishing 2014 by Dr. Brown's Apps, LLC, Martin, Tennessee

ISBN-13: **978-1496172280**

www.drbrownsapps.com

Disclaimer
These ABA programs are designed as guidelines for parents and caregivers of children with behavioral problems and developmental delays associated with neuropsychological disorders, such as autism, and are not a substitute for direct consultation by a psychologist or behavior analyst. (Go to www.bacb.com to locate Board Certified Behavior Analyst in your area.) If your child has compliance problems, tantrums, self-injurious behavior, or psychiatric problems, a licensed psychologist or psychiatrist should be consulted.

CONTENTS

Preface	1
Chapter 1 - Introduction	3
Types of Disorders	4
Overview	6
Ten Tips for Managing Behavioral Problems	11
Chapter 2 - Programs	12
1 Establishing Eye Contact *(With Bonus)*	13
2 Following Directions	17
3 Eliminating Tantrums & Screaming *(With Bonus)*	21
4 Eliminating Aggressive Behavior	26
5 Eliminating Self-Injurious Behavior	29
6 Behavior in Stores and Restaurants	33
7 Increasing Compliance	35
8 Desensitizing to Loud Noises	37
9 Toilet Training	39
10 Teach Shapes, Colors, Numbers, Letters	42
11 Establishing Verbal Behavior *(With Bonus)*	46
12 Eliminating Chewing on Objects and Pica	50

13	Modeling Appropriate Behavior	52
14	Eliminating Separation Anxiety	54
15	Eliminating Attention Deficits	57
16	Controlling Hyperactivity	59
17	Shaping Independent Play	61
18	Eliminating Self-Stimulatory Behavior	63
19	Eliminating Echolalia	66
20	Eliminating Repetitive Vomiting	68
21	Increasing Social Behavior	70
22	Listening and Remembering Directions	73
23	Reducing Frustration	75
24	Sleep Cycle Problems	77
25	The Child Who Says "No"	81
Chapter 3 – Mini-Programs		85
1	Teaching Children to Share	86
2	Teaching a Child to Sit Still	87
3	Relaxing a Child Who is Upset	88
4	Teaching a Child to Stop	89
5	Teaching a Child to Hurry Up	90

PREFACE

Ideally, children with autism or other neuropsychological disorders, such as those listed in the Table of Contents, need to be under the care of a pediatrician experienced in the treatment of neuropsychological disorders and also need to be evaluated and followed by a pediatric neurologist. Additional evaluations and treatment by occupational therapists, physical therapists, speech language pathologists, and psychologists are usually necessary as well. (Many kids with neuropsychological disorders do not make eye contact or follow directions. Parents often wonder if there is something wrong with their child's hearing. Usually, this is not the case, but these kids do need a hearing evaluation just to make sure.)

Unfortunately, what kids with neuropsychological disorders need and what they get are usually two different things, with their needs being lost in the politics of special education and managed health care. Many families in rural areas, as well as families in urban areas, do not get the services they so desperately need. Applied Behavioral Analysis (ABA) and a handful of prescription drugs are the most effective ways to manage behavior problems in children with neuropsychological disorders. And if it is at all possible, you should contact an ABA therapist in your area for help. (Go to www.bacb.com to locate ABA therapists.) Find someone experienced in working with children who have the same diagnosis as your child.

Of course, this costs money, and special education supervisors and managed health care moguls are tight-fisted, especially when it comes to behavioral problems. If you have to go it alone, try the ABA programs in my ABA book. For the last thirty years in my clinic, I have been giving these guidelines to parents, teachers, and other caregivers. These basic ABA programs are 2 to 5 pages in length, double-spaced, simple to use and easy to understand, and will usually eliminate the child's behavioral problems in a short period of time. Occasionally, small modifications have to be made in the ABA programs for a particular child.

Many parents and caregivers think ABA programs are too simplistic to work on their child's complicated neuropsychological disorder, but don't be misled, ABA programs work, although they do require a lot of effort and patience and a lot of money if you visit an ABA psychologist in his office--$75--$150 per hour. (Many of the

ABA programs in my book are also effective for normally developing children with behavioral problems.)

ABA programs require baseline measures of the behavioral problem (either a count or a time measure of the behavioral problem during the assessments) before we introduce a behavioral intervention. We then continue to monitor the occurrence of the behavioral problem during the intervention, and we usually know after a week or two whether the ABA behavioral intervention is working. If for some reason there is not a significant change from baseline after two weeks, then you modify the program, as suggested. (See Overview)

Note: This is not a book that should be read cover to cover. The chapter on an Overview of Behavioral Assessments, Behavioral Interventions, and Maintenance and Generalization of Behavioral Changes should be read before any of the ABA programs are implemented and it is a good idea to also go through my online ABA course.

Note: Caregivers will notice a certain redundancy if they read very many of my Applied Behavioral Analysis (ABA) programs. Of course, different ABA programs target different behavioral problems, but there is still that repetition that pops up in program after program. Perhaps that is why ABA programs work so well for kids with autism and other neuropsychological disorders. We also provide individual ABA programs to caregivers as well as my ABA e-Book so again the redundancy.

CHAPTER 1 INTRODUCTION

The following pages contain a quick introduction to some of the disorders you may be facing, an overview of the programs in this book, and some quick tips for dealing with some common problems.

Section 1
Types of Neuropsychological Disorders in Children

Approximately half of the children who come to my clinic now are diagnosed with one of the Autism Spectrum Disorders, such as Rhett's Disorder, Pervasive Developmental Disorder Not Otherwise Specified, or just plain Autism. And that is not surprising. Autism is in the news now, reportedly increasing at epidemic rates.

The rest of the children who come to my clinic have some other neuropsychological disorder, such as one of those listed below, or some times rare disorders such as Aarskog Syndrome or Alternating Hemiplegia of Childhood (see www.rarediseases.org). More commonly, a child comes in who has obvious neurological problems, but no diagnosis can be made.

No matter what the diagnosis or lack of, most of these children have compliance problems when they first come in and parents and other caregivers do not know which behaviors are related to the syndromes and which behaviors are simply noncompliant behaviors. In order to deal with the behaviors related to the syndromes, it is usually necessary to first manage the behaviors having to do with compliance. The first ABA programs we run in our clinic almost always have to do with compliance issues, such as making eye contact, following directions consistently, and eliminating behaviors that interfere with compliance, such as tantrums, aggressive behavior, or self-injurious behavior. Then ABA programs dealing with specific problems, such as attention deficits, etc., are implemented. Having your child compliant and under verbal control is also important so other therapists can work effectively with your child.

Additional information and ABA programs for the behavioral problems listed below and in an online ABA course for caregivers can be found at: www.childrenstreatmentcenter4autism.com and www.drbrownsapps.com

Neuropsychological Disorders (with links)

Disorder	Link
Fragile X Syndrome	wikipedia.org/wiki/Fragile_X_syndrome
Mental Retardation	wikipedia.org/wiki/Mental_Retardation#Terminology
Learning Disorders	wikipedia.org/wiki/Learning_disorders
Language Delays	wikipedia.org/wiki/Language_delay
Williams Syndrome	wikipedia.org/wiki/Williams_Syndrome
Attention-Deficit-Hyperactivity Disorder	wikipedia.org/wiki/Attention_deficit_hyperactivity_disorder
Feeding and Eating Disorders of Infancy or Early Childhood	wikipedia.org/wiki/Feeding_disorder
Tic Disorders, including Tourette's Disorder	wikipedia.org/wiki/Tic#Tic_disorders
Elimination Disorders	www.minddisorders.com/Del-Fi/Elimination-disorders.html
Separation Anxiety Disorder	wikipedia.org/wiki/Separation_Anxiety_Disorder
Selective Mutism	wikipedia.org/wiki/Selective_Mutism
Fetal Alcohol Syndrome	wikipedia.org/wiki/Fetal_Alcohol_Syndrome
Prenatal Cocaine Exposure (Crack Babies)	wikipedia.org/wiki/Crack_babies
Failure to Thrive Syndrome	wikipedia.org/wiki/Failure_to_thrive
Down Syndrome	wikipedia.org/wiki/Down_Syndrome
Traumatic Brain Injury	wikipedia.org/wiki/Traumatic_Brain_Injury
Shaken Baby Syndrome	wikipedia.org/wiki/Shaken_Baby_Syndrome
Cerebral Palsy	wikipedia.org/wiki/Cerebral_Palsy
Lesch-Nyhan Syndrome	wikipedia.org/wiki/Lesch-Nyhan_Syndrome
Prader-Willi Syndrome	wikipedia.org/wiki/Prader-Willi_Syndrome
Angelman Syndrome	wikipedia.org/wiki/Angelman_Syndrome
Tuberous Sclerosis	wikipedia.org/wiki/Tuberous_Sclerosis
Sleep Disorders	wikipedia.org/wiki/Sleep_disorders
Psychiatric Disorders	wikipedia.org/wiki/Psychiatric_disorders
Miscellaneous Genetic Disorders and Inborn Errors of Metabolism	wikipedia.org/wiki/Newborn_screening

Section 2
Overview

Overview of ABA Behavioral Assessments, Behavioral Interventions, and Maintenance and Generalization of Behavioral Changes

Defining behavior in behavioral terms, taking baseline measures, noting the antecedents and consequences of behavior, starting a behavioral intervention to change behavior, and maintaining behavioral changes are covered.

After reading the overview, select, from the list in the Table of Contents, the behavioral problems you wish to work on first with your child. Children with neuropsychological disorders often have numerous behavioral problems, and the order that you take up the behavioral problems is important.

Eye contact on command is the first problem you will want to deal with if your child is not making consistent eye contact and seems unaware of what is going on around him/her. After your child is making eye contact reliably, then move to following directions. Many children who do not follow directions are also aggressive, have tantrums, or engage in self-injurious behavior when given a direction. The ABA program for <u>following directions</u> can be combined with the

ABA programs for aggressive behavior, self-injurious behavior, or tantrums, and run at the same time.

Once you have your child making eye contact, following one-step directions 90% of the time, and have eliminated aggressive behavior, self-injurious behavior, and tantrums, you are ready to start working on your child's developmental delays. And remember--your child often engages in negative behavior just to get your attention. Try to focus on and reinforce appropriate behavior in your child. As appropriate behavior increases, inappropriate behavior will decrease. You "reap what you sow" with kids.

Behavioral Assessments:

Every Applied Behavioral Analysis (ABA) program begins with a behavioral assessment. This insures the right match between the behavioral intervention and the specific behavioral problems in the child. In the behavioral assessment we want to accomplish four things:

1. Define the child's behavioral problem in behavioral terms.
2. Take a baseline of how often or long the child's behavioral problem occurs.
3. Note the antecedents of the child's behavioral problem.
4. Note the consequences of the child's behavioral problem.

Defining the behavioral problem in behavioral terms simply means that we are going to find a way to count the frequency or time the occurrence of the behavioral problem whenever we observe it. For example, if a parent says a child is aggressive, this is not a behavioral term. We cannot see or measure the aggression. However, if a parent says a child hits a sibling, then this is a behavioral term. We can see the child hit a sibling and count the frequency that the child hits a sibling.

A baseline is a representative sample of the behavioral problem over a short period of time--for example, the number of tantrums the child has each day or how long the child stays on task. Once we have a baseline, we will begin our behavioral intervention and continue to monitor the frequency with which the behavioral problem occurs. After a reasonable period of time, we can then compare changes in the frequency of the behavioral problem to the baseline to see if our behavioral intervention is working. Obviously, if the behavioral intervention is not working for some reason, then we will try something else.

Noting the antecedents of the behavioral problem: Keep a diary of what happens immediately before the behavioral problem occurs. For example, if a child tantrums after a parent says "no," then the parent saying "no" is an antecedent condition.

Noting the consequences of the behavioral problem: Include in your diary what happens to the child as a result of the behavioral problem. In the above example, if the child tantrums after being told "no" and the parent gives in, then the parent giving in is the consequence. (Now what do you think the child will do the next time the parent says "no"?)

Children, with or without neuropsychological disorders, learn how to behave as a result of what happens to them. If the parent says "no," the child learns by experience (consequences) that a tantrum will let him/her get his/her way. So a behavioral intervention simply teaches a child a new, appropriate way of behaving.

More specific information on behavioral assessments can be found at the beginning of each behavioral problem listed below. I have attached a copy of the record-keeping form I give parents who come to my clinic. I ask them to count the frequency of the inappropriate behavior, or in some cases time its occurrence, and keep a diary of antecedents and consequences at the bottom of the page and on the back. Specific directions for defining specific behavioral problems in behavioral terms, taking baselines, and noting antecedents and consequences are provided with each ABA program.

I have also attached a copy of a record form filled out with an example of a child who tantrums. For the baseline, the number of tantrums are tallied each day for seven days and the antecedents and consequences of each tantrum are recorded at the bottom. The behavioral intervention will then be introduced and the number of tantrums that occur that week will be compared to the baseline. If there is a decline, then we know the ABA program is working. (Blank forms for monitoring behavior, both quantitatively as well as qualitatively, are found at the end of each ABA program. These should be filled out as instructed.)

See Unit III of my online course for more information on behavioral assessments.

Behavioral Interventions:
Diagnostic and Statistical Manual of Mental Disorders (DSM-IV or DSM-V): The provider of your child's health services may have given you a DSM-IV or DSM-V classification such as Autism, Pervasive Developmental Disorder, Conduct Disorder, etc. This simply means that your child's problems fit into a syndrome (collection of symptoms) and a label has been coined to describe the syndrome. Often the same behavioral problems are found in a number of different DSM syndromes. For example, children diagnosed with a number of syndromes do not follow directions and have tantrums.

When we think about behavioral problems in children, we tend to think of behavioral excesses, such as aggressive behavior or temper tantrums. Not so obvious are behavioral deficits, which are appropriate behaviors that do not occur in the child or occur at a very low frequency. Examples of behavioral deficits are: attention deficits; not following directions; elective mutes; lacking age-appropriate skills, such as being toilet trained; lacking appropriate dressing and feeding behaviors, etc.; failure to imitate; motivation problems; shyness; cooperative play; depression; hypoactivity; and withdrawal.

Some other examples of behavioral excesses are: excessive crying; hyperactivity; stereotypical repetitive movements or ritualistic behaviors, such as rocking; self-injurious behaviors, such as head banging; tics; phobias; lying; and stealing.

Generally speaking, if we have a behavioral excess, then we want to choose a behavioral intervention to decrease it. And if we have a behavioral deficit, we want to choose a behavioral intervention to increase it.

In managing kids with neuropsychological disorders, we also need to be especially careful noting children who have "learned to be helpless." In other words, their social environment has reinforced helpless behavior. More attention (reinforcement) is given to the child who does not perform an appropriate behavior than one to who does.

See Units IV through IX of my online course for more information about behavioral interventions.

When you consider using the various behavioral interventions suggested in the

ABA programs targeting specific problems, use good judgment. For example, if your child is diabetic or has food allergies, do not use candy as a reinforcer. If your child will not go to time out when you tell him/her to and is too large for you to take him/her there without risk of injury, then consider some other procedure. Always think about safety first. You know your child better than anyone else.

Maintenance and Generalization of Behavioral Changes

Once we have intervened and changed the child's behavior successfully, then we want to make sure the behavioral change is permanent and generalizes to other situations. Procedures for accomplishing this are included at the end of each ABA program.

See Unit X of my online course for more information on maintenance and generalization.

Forms:

Most chapters need a record keeping form to help measure and improve your child's progress. All of the forms are in PDF format and have been zipped up and placed on our server. Please go to the link below to download and print out your forms:

- http://files.drbrownsapps.com/

Any time you see the following icon, it means that there is a form available for you to use in that chapter. Beside the icon will be the name of the document that you should print out and use for that chapter.

Section 3
Ten Tips for Managing Behavioral Problems in Children

1. When you are holding the hand of a toddler and walking along, sometimes the toddler will fall to the ground. This is likely to happen in a store when the child does not want to leave or in a parking lot. Bend your knees so you won't hurt your back, and grab the toddler by the arm closest to you. Wrap your other arm around the child and with your hand on the child's stomach stand up, and carry the child by your side, face down, like a sack of potatoes. Most children do not like to be in this position, and after a few experiences of being carried like this, will stop falling to the ground.
2. Some children with autism are tactile defensive and do not like to be touched. However, deep muscle massage may be reinforcing for these children.
3. Children with autism or other neuropsychological disorders who run when you try to approach them will often let you get close if you move toward them at 45-degree angles.
4. When working with children who are tactile defensive, move slowly and tell them what you are going to do before you do it.
5. Usually, it is best to only run 1 or 2 ABA programs at a time. However, if a child does not follow directions and/or throws a tantrum, engages in aggression or self-injurious behavior when given a direction, then all of these programs can be run at one time.
6. Establish compliance in your child using the appropriate ABA programs, before you use the ABA programs that target developmental delays.
7. Always emphasize the positive part of the ABA program and not just the negative.
8. Kids always are their worst when you get on the phone or have company over. Have someone call you periodically during the day and hang up. Pretend you are talking to them. If your child acts up, put him/her in time out. Similarly, have a friend over whom you do not mind leaving while you put your child in time out. Of course, if the child is good while you are on the phone or when company is over, reinforce him/her with some tangible reinforcer and praise.
9. Do not discuss or argue with other caregivers about an ABA program in front of the child. Be united and consistent.
10. Always explain the ABA program to the child before you begin.

CHAPTER 2 PROGRAMS

The following sections contain 25 ABA programs plus additional bonus content. Eye contact on command is the first problem you will want to deal with if your child is not making consistent eye contact and seems unaware of what is going on around him/her. After your child is making eye contact reliably, then move to following directions. See the overview for more information.

Program 1: Establishing Eye Contact

Children with various neuropsychological disorders, such as autism, may not make eye contact on command or they may not even make spontaneous eye contact. Many parents complain that their child never looks at them or acknowledges their presence. Obviously, a child has to make eye contact with caregivers, as well as peers, in order to learn. This is often the first ABA program I give parents of children diagnosed with autism or pervasive developmental disorder, as well as other children who do not make eye contact

Behavioral Assessment

Each day, say your child's name followed by "look at me." Do this every five minutes for one hour and note whether or not the child makes eye contact. When you say the child's name and the phrase "look at me," only say it one time in a firm voice, but do not shout, or have a pleading tone in your voice. Try to say the direction like you have every expectation that your child will make eye contact with you. Do this for five-seven days. Do not stop if the frequency or time measure is trending upward or downward. In other words, we want a representative sample before we begin intervention.

Behavioral Intervention

After you have completed the assessment, repeat the same procedure, except this time reinforce any slight turn of the child's head in your direction or a quick shift of the child's eyes in your general direction. Reinforce these eye contact approximations immediately. A Tupperware bowl full of bite size goodies is what we use as tangible reinforcers for most kids, plus praise, clapping, pats on the back, tickling, etc. You may know some other reinforcer that works with your child. Do not worry. We are not going to be reinforcing approximations to eye contact or actual eye contact with bite-size goodies for long. But this is the way you have to start with these kids. If there are no approximations to eye contact, you will have to use a prompt to get your child to look at you on command. Hold a favorite toy in front of your child's face when you ask your child to look at you. Then slowly move the toy until it is in front of your face and your child is looking at you and the toy. Keep a careful count each day of approximations or eye contacts with prompts so you can see how your child is progressing.

Do not ask your child to make eye contact more often than once every five minutes for one hour a day. However, if you notice your child is making spontaneous eye contact with you, lavishly praise your child and give a reinforcer. Be sure to tell your child what the reward is for each time.

One of our additional goals here is to get your child under verbal control. It is best at this time if you do not talk excessively. We want the child to learn that, when he or she hears someone talking, it is best to look and listen. Excessive talking is going to slow us down.

Once you have the child making approximations to eye contact, then withhold reinforcement until a closer approximation is made. If you are using a toy as a prompt, hold the toy in front of your face and require longer and longer periods of eye contact. Then begin to move the toy slowly toward your face when you ask the child to make eye contact and see if you can get eye contact without moving the toy all the way in front of your face. You should see an increase in both spontaneous eye contact and eye contact on command in several days.

If there is not a significant change from baseline after two weeks, contact a psychologist versed in ABA in your area, if at all possible. (Go to www.bacb.com to locate ABA therapists.) One possibility for the ABA program not working is satiation; in other words, your child is getting tired of or does not like whatever goodies you are using as reinforcers. Try something different. And be sure everyone is following the ABA program.

Maintenance and Generalization

Once you have a noticeable change from baseline, continue to deliver social reinforcement (in the form of praise, hugs, or pats on the back) as often as you can following appropriate eye contact. Edible reinforcers, such as candy or other treats, may be faded out once a significant change from baseline is achieved. Only give the tangible reinforcer every other time, then every third time, etc. until it is no longer required to maintain appropriate behavior. Of course, social reinforcement should still be given as often as possible.

Note: Some children start making eye contact, then go through periods of refusing to make eye contact on command even though eye contact has been established. When this happens, put the child in time out and sit beside the child. Tell the child that he/she cannot get out of time out until he/she makes eye contact. When the child makes eye contact, he/she gets out of time out, but does not get a reinforcer for making eye contact.

Please use the following form:

aba_p01_eye_contact.pdf - http://files.drbrownsapps.com/

Bonus Program: Establishing Sustained Eye Contact

As I mentioned in ABA Program Number 1, Part 1, Applied Behavioral Analysis (ABA) Program for Establishing Eye Contact, children with various neuropsychological disorders, such as autism, may not make eye contact on command or they may not even make spontaneous eye contact. A related problem, especially in older children, is eye contact may be fleeting. The child may briefly glance at the parent or caregiver when asked, but then the child quickly looks away. Obviously, sustained eye contact must be made for appropriate behavior to occur.

Behavioral Assessment
Each day for five-seven days, say your child's name followed by "look at me." Do this every five minutes for one hour. Note whether or not the child makes eye contact and count the number of seconds that the child keeps making eye contact with you. When you say the child's name and the phrase "look at me," only say it one time in a firm voice, but do not shout, or have a pleading tone in your voice. Try to say the direction like you have every expectation that your child will make eye contact with you. Do not prompt the child to continue making eye contact. Do this for five-seven days. Do not stop if the frequency or time measure is trending upward or downward. In other words, we want a representative sample before we begin intervention. If your child fails to make eye contact on command more than 50% of the time, implement Part 1 of ABA Program Number 1 for establishing eye contact. Once you have established eye contact on command, then run this ABA program.

Behavioral Intervention
On Day Six (or Eight), repeat the same procedure, except this time

verbally prompt your child one time, before he or she looks away, to keep looking at you. Reinforce any slight increase in the length of eye contact immediately. A Tupperware bowl full of bite size goodies, such as M&M's, chips, Froot Loops, Cheerios, (the child only gets to pick one) is what we use for most kids, plus praise, clapping, pats on the back, tickling, etc. You may know some other reinforcer that works with your child. Do not worry, we are not going to be reinforcing increases in the length of eye contact with bite-size goodies for long, but this is the way you have to start with these kids.

Gradually, require more and more time looking at you for the reinforcer, but do not use more than one verbal prompt. Do not ask your child to make sustained eye contact more often than once every five minutes for one hour a day. A Tupperware bowl full of bite size goodies, such as M&M's, chips, Froot Loops, Cheerios, (the child only gets to pick one) is what we use for most kids. If you notice your child is making spontaneous sustained eye contact with you, lavishly praise your child and give a reinforcer. Be sure to tell your child what the reward is for each time.

Once you have the child making eye contact for a reasonable period of time, begin fading the verbal prompt. Use the verbal prompt every other time, and if there is no reduction in the length of eye contact, use the verbal prompt every fourth time and so on until it is eliminated.

If there is not a significant change from baseline after two weeks, contact a psychologist versed in ABA in your area if at all possible. (Go to www.bacb.com to locate ABA therapists.) One possibility for the ABA program not working is satiation; in other words, your child is getting tired of or does not like whatever goodies you are using as a reinforcer. Try something different. And be sure everyone is following the ABA program.

Maintenance and Generalization

Once you have a noticeable change from baseline, continue to deliver social reinforcement (in the form of praise, hugs, or pats on the back) as often as you can following appropriate eye contact. Edible reinforcers, such as candy or other treats, may be faded out once a significant change from baseline is achieved. Only give the tangible reinforcer every other time, then every third time, etc. until it is no longer required to maintain appropriate behavior. Of course, social reinforcement should still be given as often as possible.

Please use the following form:

 aba_p01b_eye_contact.pdf - http://files.drbrownsapps.com/

Program 2: Increasing the Number of Directions Followed by a Child

Children with neuropsychological disorders need to be compliant and follow directions. Otherwise, it is impossible to determine accurately the child's level of functioning. If a child does not follow directions from teachers and other professionals, then it is often assumed that the child is incapable of doing what is asked because of the deficits associated with his/her neuropsychological disorder. Many children with neuropsychological disorders do not reach their full potential simply because they are non-compliant and do not follow directions.

Behavioral Assessment
Each day, for five-seven days, give your child a one-step direction every five minutes for one hour. The direction should be something you already know the child can do. Record the number of times your child follows the direction. ("No" is a direction for the child to stop doing something and should be included as one of the directions.) Do this for five-seven days. Do not stop if the frequency or time measure is trending upward or downward. In other words, we want a representative sample before we begin intervention

Behavioral Intervention
Day Six (or Eight): Before you give the child a direction, first, say the child's name in a firm tone. Then give the direction also in a firm tone. Be sure you have the child's attention. In this program, attention = eye contact with you. If the child does not respond and make eye contact with you, clap your hands loudly and then give the direction if the child makes eye contact. If the child still does not respond and make eye contact with you, gently take the child's chin and turn his or her face toward you. Only give the command <u>once</u> and never plead or beg with the child to comply. No matter what the child is doing he/she should <u>immediately</u> comply.

If your child immediately follows the direction, praise him or her, clap, give a small piece of candy, a sip of coke or juice, whatever the child likes, and show your child that you appreciate his or her minding and doing what you ask. Occasionally, do something even more special when directions are followed. (A Tupperware bowl full of bite size goodies is what we use as tangible reinforcers for most kids in our clinic.)

Of course the child will not always comply and follow the direction. Whenever this happens, do not say anything, but immediately go get the child, tell the child that he or she is going to time out for not minding, and put the child in time out. (Do not threaten time out to get the child to follow the direction. This might work for a while, but then time out becomes less effective.)

Time out is an often used and misused procedure. If done properly, time out is a very effective, humane procedure. Find a place in your house where a time out chair, preferably a chair with arms and not a bench, can be left. The chair should face a blank wall and not be close to a window, shelves, glass, electrical outlets, or storage cabinets containing chemicals. Hallways and alcoves often work. Do not use bathrooms or closets. The time out chair should be close to the play area so the child can be placed in time out quickly. Think safety, especially for small children. (If the child is very young, then the baby bed will do, and no, the child will not develop an aversion to the baby bed and have sleep problems. An alternative time out procedure for a young toddler is to sit him/her down on the floor with his/her back to you and hold them there for thirty seconds. Do not talk to the child except to tell him or her at the beginning and end of time out why he or she is in time out.)

For young toddlers, you can just count to thirty in your head. For older children, use an egg timer and teach the child that he or she cannot get out of time out until the egg timer goes off. The child has to stay in time out for three minutes, plus one minute of good behavior. In other words, the child has to be quiet and cannot be arguing, complaining, or tantruming for one full minute before he or she can get out of time out.

Do not be surprised if the child comes up with a whole bag of new inappropriate behaviors in order to get out of time out. Kids have been known to gag, vomit, and one of my own kids even hit herself in the face several times. Do not respond and thereby reinforce these new inappropriate behaviors or they will increase in their frequency. Only good behavior gets the child out of time out.

(Initially, some kids have to be held in time out. Gradually, decrease the restraint you have on the child and make sure he/she is sitting there quietly for one minute before he/she gets out. If the child is too large to safely hold in time out, then use a response cost procedure instead. In response cost something the child values is taken away temporarily. Examples include watching TV, going outside, videos, the opportunity to play games with caregivers, favorite foods or beverages, a favorite toy, etc.)

In the beginning of this procedure, it is not unusual for a child to be in time out for fifteen to twenty minutes before he/she quiets down, and to go to time out as often as twenty times a day. After a few days, the child learns the requirements of the time out procedure and he/she gets out in the minimum four minutes. The number of times the child goes to time out each day also drops dramatically. (Record the frequency and length of time outs on the form provided and you will see the child's progress.)

When the child gets out of time out, remind your child of why he or she had to go to time out in a firm tone. Tell your child that he/she will have to go again if your directions are not followed immediately. Do not be timid with your voice or body language.

Note: The time out procedure above is repeated in many, but not all of the ABA programs in this volume. There has been much written about time out procedures, but I have found that this is the most effective procedure for most kids.

Everybody who cares for the child has to follow this procedure. Try to concentrate on the positive part of the program and not just the negative.

If there is not a significant change from baseline after two weeks, contact a psychologist versed in ABA in your area, if at all possible. (Go to www.bacb.com to locate ABA therapists.) One possibility for the ABA program not working is satiation. In other words, your child is getting tired of whatever reinforcer you are using. Try something different. And be sure everyone is following the ABA program.

Maintenance and Generalization

Continue to deliver social reinforcement in the form of praise, hugs, pats on the back, etc. as often as you can following appropriate behavior. Edible reinforcers, such as candy or other treats, may be faded out once a significant change from baseline is achieved. Only give the tangible reinforcer every other time, then every third time, etc. until it is no longer required to maintain appropriate behavior. Of course, social reinforcement should be given as often as possible. If your child tantrums, becomes aggressive, engages in self-injurious behavior, or any other misbehavior when given a direction, then combine the ABA programs for these behaviors with the ABA program for following directions.

Please use the following form:

aba_p02_directions.pdf- http://files.drbrownsapps.com/

Program 3: Eliminating Tantrums and Screaming

Toddlers, and even some older children, throw tantrums and scream. Usually, the tantrum is in response to frustration over not being able to do something because the toddler's sensory, cognitive, or motor systems have not adequately developed, or the caregiver stops the toddler from doing something because he/she is engaging in a behavior that could be inappropriate or even dangerous. If the parent completely ignores every tantrum, the child will learn how to cope on his or her own and the tantrums will disappear. However, many caregivers give in to the child when he/she tantrums and the child learns that tantrums are a way to control people.

Often children with neuropsychological disorders have an additional problem. The neurological mechanisms that control tantrums are not functioning and they cannot control themselves when they become frustrated. This problem needs to be handled somewhat differently.

Behavioral Assessment

Record the number of tantrums and/or screaming episodes your child has each day, and note antecedent conditions (what happens immediately before the tantrum) and consequences (what happens to the child following the tantrum). For example, does the child get his way? Do this for five-seven days. Do not stop if the frequency or time measure is trending upward or downward. In other words, we want a representative sample before we begin intervention

Behavioral Intervention

Day Six (or Eight): To eliminate tantrums, we need to set up a reinforcement procedure and a time out procedure. Look at the antecedents of your child's tantrums. If you find that the child tantrums when frustrated while trying to perform a particular activity, then give a reinforcer, such as a bite size piece of candy, immediately before he/she gets frustrated. (A Tupperware bowl full of bite size goodies is what we use as tangible reinforcers for most kids in our clinic.) Tell the child why he is getting the reward. (Do not worry we are going to fade out or slowly eliminate edible rewards once we have eliminated tantrums.)

If your assessment indicates that your child has a tantrum every hour or so for numerous reasons, then set up a reinforcement contingency and give the child a tangible reward, such as a cookie, every fifty minutes if the child does not tantrum. If you prefer, play a game with the child, watch a video, or do anything the child enjoys. Again, be sure to tell the child that the reward is for not having a tantrum.

When your child does tantrum, act quickly. Intervene at the very beginning of the tantrum and the behavioral intervention will work better. Tell the child that he or she is going to time out for having a tantrum and put the child in time out immediately. (Do not threaten time out to get the child to stop tantruming. This might work for a while, but then time out becomes less effective.)

Time out is an often used and misused procedure. If done properly, time out is a very effective, humane procedure. Find a place in your house where a time out chair, preferably a chair with arms and not a bench, can be left. The chair should face a blank wall and not be close to a window, shelves, glass, electrical outlets, or storage cabinets containing chemicals. Hallways and alcoves often work. Do not use bathrooms or closets. The time out chair should be close to the play area so the child can be placed in time out quickly. Think safety, especially for small children. (If the child is very young, then the baby bed will do, and no, the child will not develop an aversion to the baby bed and have sleep problems. An alternative procedure for a young toddler is to sit him/her down on the floor with his/her back to you and hold him/her there for thirty seconds. Do not talk to the child except to tell him or her at the beginning and end of time out why they are in time out.)

For the young toddler you can just count to thirty in your head. For an older child, use an egg timer and teach the child that he or she does not get out of time out until the egg timer goes off. The child has to stay in time out for three minutes plus one minute of good behavior. In other words, the child has to be quiet and cannot be arguing/complaining/tantruming/etc. for one full minute in order to get out of time out.

Do not be surprised if the child comes up with a whole bag of new inappropriate behaviors in order to get out of time out. Kids have been known to gag, vomit, and one of my own kids hit herself in the face several times. Do not respond and thereby reinforce these new inappropriate behaviors or they will increase in their frequency. Only good behavior gets the child out of time out. (Initially, some kids have to be held in time out. Gradually, decrease the restraint you have on the child and make sure he/she is sitting there quietly for one minute before he/she gets out. If the child is too large to hold in time out then use a response cost procedure instead. In response cost something the child values is taken away temporarily. Examples include: watching TV, going outside, videos, the opportunity to play games with caregivers, favorite foods or beverages, a favorite toy, etc.)

In the beginning of the intervention program, it's not unusual for a child to be in time out for fifteen to twenty minutes before he/she quiets down and to go to time out as often as twenty times a day. After a few days, the child learns the requirements of the time out procedure and he/she is out in the minimum four minutes. The number of times the child goes to time out each day also drops dramatically. (Record the frequency and length of time outs on the form provided and you can see your child's progress.)

When the child gets out of time out, remind him/her of why he/she had to go to time out in a firm tone. Tell your child he or she will have to go again whenever tantrums occur.

Note: The time out procedure above is repeated in many, but not all of the ABA programs in this volume. There has been much written about time out, but I have found that this is the most effective procedure for most kids.

Everybody who cares for the child has to follow this procedure. Try to concentrate on the positive reinforcement part of the program and not just the negative time out part of the program. Do not be timid with your voice or body language.

If there is not a significant change from baseline after two weeks, contact a psychologist versed in ABA in your area, if at all possible. (Go to www.bacb.com to locate ABA therapists.) One possibility for the ABA program not working is satiation. In other words, your child is getting tired of whatever reinforcer you are using. Try something different and be sure everyone is following the ABA program. In rare cases medication is required along with the ABA program to eliminate tantrums. A pediatric neurologist should be consulted.

Maintenance and Generalization

As before, continue to deliver social reinforcement in the form of praise, hugs, pats on the back, etc. as often as you can once tantrums have decreased. Edible reinforcers, such as candy or other treats, may be faded out once a significant change from baseline is achieved. Only give the edible reinforcer every other time, then every third time, etc. until it is no longer required to maintain appropriate behavior. Of course, social reinforcement should be given as often as possible. If your child tantrums when given a direction, then see ABA Program Number 2. and run both ABA programs at the same time.

Please use the following form:

aba_p03_tantrums.pdf- http://files.drbrownsapps.com/

Bonus Program: Decreasing Colicky Crying in Infants

According to the literature there is no known physiological, anatomical, or medical cause of colicky crying. Several studies have put to rest the gas myth. Colicky babies have no more gas than babies who are not colicky; they just cry excessively. Colic does not appear to be something a baby has, but something a baby does. The program below stops excessive crying.

Behavioral Assessment

For the baseline, time how long your baby cries in a typical hour. If you baby cries for longer than an hour at a time, use a two-hour period.

Behavioral Intervention
1. Buy or make a recording of "soothing music." For some reason, female vocalists seem to work best. Keep the music on when your child is awake and silent for at least thirty seconds. Interact with your child at these times - - talk to him or her, hold him or her, rock your child, be affectionate and loving.
2. As soon as your child starts to cry, turn off the music and attend to the child's needs like changing or feeding, but do not talk.
3. If your child continues to cry after you have taken care of all of his/her needs, put the child in an infant carrier. The child should stay in the infant carrier for 3-5 minutes--longer if the child continues to cry.
4. Once the child stops crying for 30 seconds turn on the music, and repeat Step 1.
5. This procedure works, sometimes quickly and sometimes slowly. Continue to time your child's crying as you did in the baseline, in case the decrease is gradual. Keep a record of your baby's crying in case the decrease is gradual. Follow this procedure closely and do not give up. If you "reinforce" your baby's crying by picking it up even once, it will set you back.

Please use the following form:

aba_p03b_crying.pdf- http://files.drbrownsapps.com/

Program 4: Eliminating Aggressive Behavior in Children

Young children often engage in aggressive behavior, such as pushing, hitting, kicking, pulling hair, spitting, and biting, in day care and other group settings. Aggressive behavior may also be directed at family members and other caregivers. Nonverbal children with neuropsychological disorders may use aggression to "communicate" and control their social environment.

Behavioral Assessment

Record each biting, hitting, kicking, pushing, spitting, hair-pulling incident and note the antecedent conditions (what happens immediately before the aggressive behavior occurs) and the consequences (what immediately happens to the child when he or she is aggressive towards someone else). Do this for five-seven days. Do not stop if the frequency or time measure is trending upward or downward. In other words, we want a representative sample before we begin intervention.

Behavioral Intervention

Look at the antecedents and consequences of the child's aggressive behavior. Usually, the child is in a conflict situation, such as fighting over a toy, and aggressive behavior gets the child what he or she wants. In order to eliminate aggressive behavior, we need to set up a reinforcement contingency to reward periods or situations when aggressive behavior does not occur and a time out contingency to manage aggressive behavior when it does occur.

If your child does not engage in aggressive behavior in situations that would normally cause aggressive behavior, then deliver a reinforcer immediately. Accompany the reinforcer with praise and hugs. Let the child know that resolving conflict in ways that do not involve aggressive behavior is what you want. On the other hand, if your child is aggressive toward another child, then send the child to time out. Act quickly. Intervene at the beginning of the aggressive episode and the behavioral intervention will work better. Tell the child that he or she is going to time out for aggressive behavior (be specific) and put the child in time out. (Do not threaten time out to get the child to stop aggressive behavior. This might work for a while, but then time out becomes less effective.)

Time out is an often used and misused procedure. If done properly, time out is a very effective, humane procedure. Find a place in your house where a time out chair, preferably a chair with arms and not a bench, can be left. The chair should face a blank wall and not be close to a window, shelves, glass, electrical outlets, or storage cabinets containing chemicals. Hallways and alcoves often work. Do not use bathrooms or closets. The time out chair should be close to the play area so the child can be placed in time out quickly. Think safety, especially for small children. (If the child is very young, then the baby bed will do, and no, the child will not develop an aversion to the baby bed and have sleep problems. An alternative procedure for a young toddler is to sit him/her down on the floor with his/her back to you and hold him/her there for thirty seconds. Do not talk to the child except to tell him or her why he/she is in time out.)

For the older child, use an egg timer. He/she is to stay in time out for three minutes plus one minute of good behavior. In other words, the child has to be quiet and cannot be arguing, complaining, tantruming, or biting himself/herself, etc. for one full minute.

Do not be surprised if the child comes up with whole bag of new inappropriate behaviors in order to get out of time out. Kids have been known to gag, vomit, and one of my own kids hit herself in the face several times. Do not respond and thereby reinforce these new inappropriate behaviors or they will increase in their frequency. Only good behavior gets the child out of time out. (Initially, some kids have to be held in time out. Gradually, decrease the restraint you have on the child and make sure he/she is sitting there quietly for one minute before he/she gets out. If the child is too large to safely hold in time out, then use a response cost procedure instead. In response cost something the child values is taken away temporarily. Examples include: watching TV, going outside, videos, the opportunity to play games with caregivers, favorite foods or beverages, a favorite toy, etc.)

In the beginning of the intervention program, it is not unusual for a child to be in time out for fifteen to twenty minutes before he/she quiets down and stops biting, and a child may go to time out as often as twenty times a day. After a few days, the child learns the requirements of the time out procedure and he/she is out in the minimum four minutes and the number of times the child goes to time out each day drops dramatically. (Record the frequency and length of time outs on the form provided, and you will see how your child is progressing.)

When the child gets out of time out, remind him/her of why he/she had to go to time out in a firm tone. Tell the child he/she will have to go again if he/she engages in biting.

Note: The time out procedure above is repeated in many, but not all, of the ABA programs in this volume. There has been much written about time out, but I have found that this is the most effective procedure for most kids.

Everybody who cares for the child has to follow this procedure. Try to concentrate on the positive part of the program and not just the negative. Do not be timid with your voice or body language.

If there is not a significant change from baseline after two weeks, contact a psychologist versed in ABA in your area, if at all possible. (Go to www.bacb.com to locate ABA therapists.) One possibility for the ABA program not working is satiation. In other words, your child is getting tired of whatever reinforcer you are using. Try something different. And be sure everyone is following the ABA program.

Maintenance and Generalization

Deliver social reinforcement in the form of praise, hugs, pats on the back, etc. as often as you can following appropriate behavior. Edible reinforcers, such as candy or other treats, may be faded out once a significant change from baseline is achieved. Only give the tangible reinforcer every other time, then every third time, etc. until it is no longer required to maintain appropriate behavior. Of course, social reinforcement should be given as often as possible.

If your child is aggressive when given a direction, then see ABA Program Number 2 and run both programs at the same time.

Please use the following form:

aba_p04_aggressive%20.pdf - http://files.drbrownsapps.com/

Program 5: Eliminating Self-Injurious Behavior: Head Banging or Biting or Hitting Oneself

Head banging in children ranges from a mild tap of the head against a pillow or carpeted floor, to severe banging of the head on hard surfaces. Biting also varies from gentle gnawing of the skin, to biting out hunks of flesh. And hitting oneself can be a gentle swat to the face or a punch hard enough to leave a bruise. In some children self-injurious behavior (SIB) is so severe that further neurological damage occurs from head banging, as well as serious infections from biting. Many children engage in SIB during a tantrum when they are not getting their way, while others develop SIB at a very early age because of a neuropsychological disorder. For example, some children with autism bang their heads against the side of the crib as soon as they are old enough to acquire head control

Behavioral Assessment

Record the number of times your child engages in SIB each day, and note the antecedent conditions (what happens immediately before the SIB) and consequences (what happens to the child as a result of the SIB). Do this for five-seven days. Do not stop if the frequency or time measure is trending upward or downward. In other words, we want a representative sample before we begin intervention

Behavioral Intervention

Usually, attention from caregivers and/or letting the child have his/her way is the consequence that maintains SIB. In order to decrease and eliminate SIB, we need to set up a reinforcement contingency for periods when SIB does not occur and a contingency to manage SIB when it does occur.

Look at the baseline. If your child, on average, goes for ten minutes without SIB, then deliver a reinforcer every eight minutes the child goes without engaging in SIB. (A Tupperware bowl full of bite size goodies is what we use as tangible reinforcers for most kids in our clinic. The child only gets to pick one bite size piece.) Accompany the reinforcer with praise and a hug and tell the child why reinforcement is being given.

If your child engages in SIB, then send him/her to time out. Act quickly. Intervene at the very beginning of the SIB and the behavioral intervention will work better. Tell the child that he or she is going to time out for SIB (be specific), and put the child in time out. (Do not threaten time out to get the child to stop SIB. This might work for a while, but then time out becomes less effective.)

Time out is an often used and misused procedure. If done properly, time out is a very effective, humane procedure. Find a place in your house where a time out chair, preferably a chair with arms and not a bench, can be left. The chair should face a blank wall and not be close to a window, shelves, glass, electrical outlets, or storage cabinets containing chemicals. Hallways and alcoves often work. Do not use bathrooms or closets. The time out chair should be close to the play area so the child can be placed in time out quickly. Think safety, especially for small children. (If the child is very young, then the baby bed will do, and no, the child will not develop an aversion to the baby bed and have sleep problems. An alternative procedure for a young toddler is to sit him/her down on the floor with his/her back to you and hold him/her there for thirty seconds. Do not talk to the child except to tell him or her of why he/she is in time out.)

For the older child, use an egg timer. He/she is to stay in time out for three minutes plus one minute of good behavior. In other words, the child has to be quiet and cannot be arguing, complaining, tantruming, engaging in SIB, etc. for one full minute.

Do not be surprised if the child comes up with new inappropriate behaviors in order to get out of time out. Kids have been known to gag, vomit, and one of my own kids hit herself in the face several times. Do not respond and thereby reinforce these new inappropriate behaviors or they will increase in their frequency. Only good behavior gets the child out of time out. (Initially, some kids have to be held in time out. Gradually, decrease the restraint you have on the child and make sure he/she is sitting there quietly for one minute before he/she gets out. If the child is too large to safely hold in time out, then use a response cost procedure instead. In response cost something the child values is taken away temporarily. Examples include: watching TV, going outside, videos, the opportunity to play games with caregivers, favorite foods or beverages, a favorite toy, etc.)

In the beginning of the intervention program, it is not unusual for a child to be in time out for fifteen to twenty minutes before he/she quiets down, and a child may go as often as twenty times a day. After a few days, the child learns the requirements of the time out procedure and he/she is out in the minimum four minutes, and the number of times the child goes to time out each day drops dramatically. (Record the frequency and length of time outs on the form provided.)

When the child gets out of time out, remind him/her of why he/she had to go to time out in a firm tone. Tell the child he/she will have to go again if he/she engages in SIB.

Note: The time out procedure above is repeated in many, but not all of the ABA programs in this volume. There has been much written about the time out procedure, but I have found that this is the most effective procedure for most kids.

Everybody who cares for the child has to follow this procedure. Try to concentrate on the positive part of the program and not just the negative. Do not be timid with your voice or body language when you give your child reinforcement or take him or her to time out.

If there is not a significant change from baseline after two weeks, contact a psychologist versed in ABA in your area, if at all possible. (Go to www.bacb.com to locate ABA therapists.) One possibility for the ABA program not working is satiation. In other words, your child is getting tired of whatever reinforcer you are using. Try something different. And be sure everyone is following the ABA program.

(A few children bang their heads and bite themselves because the pain causes the release of naturally occurring opiates in the brain called endorphins. Attention from caregivers or the child getting his or her way has no effect on the frequency of SIB in these children. Naltrexone, an opiate antagonist [blocks the activity of opiate drugs in the nervous system], is used to treat children in this group. If your child does not respond to the ABA program and there is no change from baseline after several weeks, then a pediatric neurologist should be consulted for medication.)

Maintenance and Generalization

As before, continue to deliver social reinforcement in the form of praise, hugs, pats on the back, etc. as often as you can when the child does not engage in SIB. Tangible reinforcers, such as candy or other treats, may be faded out once a self-injurious behavior is eliminated. Only give the tangible reinforcer every other time, then every third time, etc. until it is no longer required to maintain appropriate behavior. Of course, social reinforcement should be given as often as possible after tangible reinforcers are eliminated. If the child engages in self-injurious behavior when given a direction, then see ABA Program Number 2 and run both programs at the same time.

(Stephen Edelson has an excellent article on SIB at AutismBehaviorProblems-owner@yahoogroups.com)

Please use the following form:

aba_p05_injurious.pdf - http://files.drbrownsapps.com/

Program 6: Controlling Children's Behavior in Stores and Restaurants

In the class I teach in Applied Behavioral Analysis, the first assignment for the students is to go to the toy section at Wal-Mart and observe how parents manage their children. Most parents change the rules when they are in the presence of other adults, and children quickly learn to take advantage of the situation.

Behavioral Assessment:
In this case, there is no need to take your child to a store or restaurant for a period of time and note antecedent conditions (what happens before) and consequences (what happens after) or take a baseline. You should be able to think back to four or five previous occasions and remember your child's behavior. Write down what happened before the inappropriate behavior occurred and what happened after. You can use this as your assessment.

Behavioral Intervention
Do not take your child to a store or restaurant alone. Take another adult with you and start out with short trips.

If your child is good in the store or restaurant, praise him/her every few minutes. Do not try to entertain or distract the child if you think he/she is starting to get upset. Simply praise the child for good behavior. If the child is good the whole time, then give an edible treat, such as a piece of candy, when you leave the store or restaurant.

Decide ahead of time who will take the child to the car if he or she misbehaves and who will stay in the store or restaurant. At the first sign of misbehavior, take the child to the car immediately. Do not threaten to take the child to the car. Put the child in his or her car seat and ignore the child. If necessary, stand outside of the car. (Never leave the child unattended in the car.)

The car is like time out at home. Take the child back inside the store after the child spends three minutes plus one minute of good behavior in the car seat. If the child misbehaves, then it's back to the car again.

Most kids do not require more than two trips to the car to get the idea. It is very important that you do not just leave the store or restaurant when your child acts up. That teaches the child that he or she is in control.

If there is not a significant change in behavior after two weeks, contact a psychologist versed in ABA in your area, if at all possible. (Go to www.bacb.com to locate ABA therapists.) One possibility for the ABA program not working is satiation. In other words, your child is getting tired of whatever reinforcer you are using. Try something different, such as another type of food or drink or some activity the child enjoys. And be sure everyone is following the ABA program.

Maintenance and Generalization

As usual, continue to deliver social reinforcement in the form of praise, hugs, and pats on the back, etc. as often as you can following appropriate behavior in the store or restaurant. Edible reinforcers, such as candy or other treats, may be faded out once a significant change from baseline is achieved. Only give the tangible reinforcer every other time, then every third time, etc. until it is no longer required to maintain appropriate behavior. Of course, social reinforcement should be given as often as possible.

Please use the following form:

aba_book/aba_p06_stores.pdf - http://files.drbrownsapps.com/

Program 7: Increasing Compliance in Children

After you have your child following directions consistently (see ABA Procedure Number 2), you can further increase compliance in your child by running the following two drills. There is no behavioral assessment. These drills are designed to establish compliance in situations where the child does not want to follow directions. This is especially important because some children with neuropsychological disorders who are not compliant fail to perform tasks they know. Teachers and other caregivers then assume the child cannot perform the task.

"Come Here" Command
Stand the child up with his/her back against the wall. Hold him or her by his/her shirt and say the child's name followed by, "come here." Gently pull the child to you. When the child gets to you, praise the child and hug him or her. Then gently push the child back against the wall and repeat 10 times. Try to use less and less force as you pull the child to you. If the child will come without pulling him or her to you, great, but always make the child come to you. Give the child a short break after the 10 trials and then repeat the drill.

An alternative way to run this drill requires two people. Get several feet apart. One person says the child's name followed by "come here." The other person holding the child gently pushes the child toward the person giving the command. As soon as the child gets there, praise the child and turn him or her around. Then the other person gives the command and the child is gently pushed toward the person who is now giving the command. As soon as the child becomes compliant, gradually increase the distance.

Both of these procedures are errorless. In other words, the child is always made to comply. Fifty times a day is a good practice target for the "come here" drill. Once you have your child coming to you reliably, run the ABA Mini Program for Teaching Your Child to Stop on Command found in Appendix 1 of this volume

Body Parts Drill

In the body parts drill, we ask the child to point to different parts of his/her body and praise him/her when he/she does so. If the child does not comply, we provide a physical prompt. Take the child's wrist and use the child's hand to point to the body part requested. Fade the physical prompts as the child begins to do the drill on his or her own. In other words, use less and less force to move the child's hand as the child becomes compliant.

This drill works well for children who are non-compliant and would rather go to time out than follow the direction. (Many children with autism fall into this category.) If the child refuses to follow a direction, do the body part drill for several minutes and then repeat the direction you first gave. Compliance should be established or re-established by this time. If not, return to the body part drill for several minutes and then give the initial direction again. Eventually, the child will follow the initial direction.

Program 8: Desensitizing a Child to Loud Noises

Children with various neuropsychological disorders are often hyperactive to loud noises, as well as other sensory stimuli. Tantrums, aggressive behavior, and self-injurious behavior are often the result of being exposed to loud noises. Desensitizing a child to loud noises or any other stimuli takes time and patience, so do not go too fast.

Behavioral Assessment
The behavioral assessment is done differently in desensitization programs.
You find the type of sound your child is most sensitive to and record it. The volume of the recording should be adjustable so that you can play it in the range from barely audible up to the level where the child becomes visibly upset. (Other dimensions of sound, such as pitch or conversation, bother some children. If this is the case, then start with the appropriate stimulus at a low level and gradually increase it as instructed below.)

Behavioral Intervention
Put the tape recorder on the opposite side of the room from the child. Give the child his or her favorite thing to eat. While the child is eating, turn on the tape recorder. The volume should be set so the

child hears the sound, and the sound arouses mild discomfort, but not enough discomfort to cause the child to get so upset that he or she cannot sit there and eat and listen to the sound. (In other words, the child should not be crying, shaking, or visibly upset.) You will have to adjust the volume and/or the distance the child is from the recorder several times in order to get this behavior.

When the child becomes relaxed, which may take one or two or many presentations, bring the tape recorder a little closer or increase the volume slightly. <u>Do not go too fast. Desensitization is a very gradual process.</u> The pleasure of eating has to override the discomfort of the noise. Of course, praise the child often for not getting upset at the noise.

As the child relaxes and seems to ignore the sound again, bring the tape recorder closer, or increase the volume. Continue this process, and eventually, the child will be able to tolerate the noise at the volume he or she is now afraid of. This will generalize to times the child is not engaged in the pleasurable activity of eating. Again, proceed slowly. If you have to decrease the volume or move the tape recorder back on some days in order keep the child relaxed, that is fine. Once the child is relaxed at that level, gradually increase the volume or bring the tape recorder closer again.

After you reach the volume level that would occur naturally and upset the child, do not go any higher. Continue at that level until the child displays no more fear of loud sounds.

This program works for all fears and phobias. Simply change the stimulus to whatever is eliciting the fear or phobia, begin desensitization at a level that will not upset the child, and gradually increase the stimulus as tolerated by the child.

Program 9: Toilet Training Children

Sigmund Freud thought that toilet training had far-reaching consequences into adulthood. It does not. However, toilet training can be a relatively easy process that takes a day or two, or it can last for months. A child that is toilet trained is better received by caregivers, daycare, and preschool programs. Unless your child is showing an interest in toilet training, wait until age two before you begin.

You should have plenty of thick cotton underwear, some bite size rewards on hand, and a potty seat that sits on the floor. If you use the toilet for training, donut inserts seem to work well for many children. However, some kids are afraid of the height and some kids actually worry about being flushed away if they fall in. All of these items should be readily available in the bathroom. Do not switch back and forth between underwear and diapers or pull-ups if you have to go some place. This greatly confuses the child and toilet training will take much longer.

Behavioral Assessment

Throughout the toilet training procedure, count the number of accidents each day and the number of times your child uses the bathroom successfully. Use the attached form so you will know how you are progressing.

Behavioral Intervention

Start this procedure when you have a day or two to devote full time to toilet training and keep the child at home. Treat toilet training like a game and do not get upset or punish your child when accidents occur. In the morning, after breakfast, take your child into the bathroom along with a favorite beverage and a supply of whatever reward you are going to use. (A Tupperware bowl full of bite size goodies is what we use as tangible reinforcers for most kids in our clinic. The child only gets to pick one bite size piece.)

Take off the child's diaper and say, "It's time to wear big boy/big girl underwear now." Let the child wear the underwear for several minutes. Then pull your child's underwear down, sit the child on the potty seat or toilet, and give the child a favorite beverage to drink. Do whatever you have to do to keep your child sitting there, drinking the beverage. As soon as the child uses the toilet successfully, praise the child and give the reward. Call in others and have them praise the child for using the toilet. Be lavish in your praise. Keep the child sitting there as long as you can and give praise and a reward every time the child uses the toilet. Continue this as long as you can. Do not force the child to sit there because we do not want to create an aversion to the toilet. We want the child to go several times in the potty and see the positive results.

When your child will no longer sit there, take away the beverage, and pull up the child's underwear. This ends phase one and we are ready for phase two. Tell the child to use the potty whenever necessary and make sure the child has easy access. If the child indicates he or she wants to use the toilet, help him/her get there as quickly as you can. Every time your child uses the toilet give praise and a reward. Do not give rewards at any other time.

Check your child every few minutes when he or she is off the toilet and ask if he or she needs to go to the toilet. If your child is dry, give praise and give a reward. If your child has an accident, which will happen, do not get upset; do not scold or punish the child. Just say, "You had an accident," change the child's clothes (the fewer clothes, the better), and continue. Many children do not know the difference between wet and dry with modern diapers, so take the child's hand and have him/her feel when they are wet or dry. Gradually increase the intervals you check or ask the child if he or she is dry if toileting successes are occurring regularly. Only give liquids occasionally and in very small amounts during this phase of training.

Continue to count the number of accidents each day and also count the number of times your child uses the toilet successfully. (At the end of one week if successes do not outnumber accidents, your child is probably not ready. Put the child back in diapers and wait a month before you try again.)

We also want to establish nighttime training at the same time as daytime training. No liquids two hours before bedtime. Do not use diapers or pull-ups at night and be sure your child can get up and use the bathroom if need be. The next morning, reward the child if he/she has not had an accident during the night. (Use a rubber sheet to protect the mattress.)

You should notice improvement the first day. If the child doesn't seem to be motivated by the same reward after awhile, try some other favorite foods. By the end of the week, I would expect your child to be trained or nearly trained. Do not worry. We are not going to continue to give rewards for using the toilet for the rest of the child's life.

Maintenance and Generalization

Continue to deliver social reinforcement as often as you can in the form of praise, hugs, pats on the back, etc. following appropriate toileting behavior. Tangible reinforcers, such as candy or other treats, may be faded out once your child is toilet trained. Only give the tangible reinforcer every other time, then every third time, etc. until it is no longer required to maintain appropriate behavior. Of course, social reinforcement should be given as often as possible. (Many children will stop asking for the reward on their own after awhile.)

Please use the following form:

aba_p09_toilet.pdf - http://files.drbrownsapps.com/

Program 10: Teach Children Shapes, Colors, Numbers, Letters, Sight Words, etc

Some children with neuropsychological disorders fail to learn different shapes, colors, numbers, or letters because of compliance problems, while other children with neuropsychological disorders do not learn because of sensory and/or neurological processing problems associated with certain disorders. If a reward is given to the child for a correct response, performance often dramatically improves in noncompliant children. On the other hand, the rate of improvement in children with actual sensory/neurological problems is much, much slower. In the beginning, the best thing to do when we are trying to teach a child to learn the differences between stimuli, such as two colors or two shapes, is to run intensive drills using bite size rewards, which we will later fade out. The rate by which the child improves tells us if we are dealing with a noncompliant child or a true sensory processing problem.

Traditional Discrete Trial Training (DTT):

If you have an iPhone, iPod Touch, or iPad skip to the section of DTT apps.)
 DTT is based on the learning principles of Applied Behavior Analysis ABA. The National Institute of Mental Health and the Surgeon General recommend Applied Behavior Analysis (ABA) as the most effective method for treating autism and related disorders. Children with Autism, ADD and ADHD, and other children who are easily distracted and have problems staying on task learn best with DTT.
 DTT works well with these children because the trials are brief and fit the short attention span and distractibility of these children. DTT keeps these children motivated because of positive reinforcement, and the behaviors learned with DTT generalize to other areas of a child's life. DTT works best if you treat it like a game. Reinforce correct responses with praise and half of a froot loop, an M&M, or some other tangible reinforcer.

Behavioral Assessment:

We will start our DTT discussion with colors, which for most children are easier to learn than shapes, letters, numbers, or sight words. Use objects, which are identical but have different colors, such as pieces of construction paper. (It's better not to use different colored toys, which the child would want to play with.) Ask the child to point to or hand you one color and record the number of correct responses, prompted responses, and incorrect responses on the attached form. Do this for several blocks of ten trials without comment or reward in order to obtain a baseline. (If you run blocks of ten trials, then it is easy to calculate the percentage of correct responses.) Only wait 3-5 seconds for a response and 3-5 seconds between trials. Be sure to switch the different colored objects from side to side so the child will not learn a position habit. (In other words, a child can learn right or left side rather than the color and still be correct. Also do not alternate the stimuli. Some kids will pick up on the alternation pattern and not learn the differences in the stimuli)

Behavioral Intervention:

After you have a baseline, reward the child immediately for each time he/she correctly picks the right color with a bite size treat. If the child gets it wrong say, "no," and ask the child again. After the child receives a "no" response twice in a row, prompt the child with the correct answer (give no reward). Point to the correct color; move it closer--anything that will make the discrimination between the two colors easier for the child. Then fade the prompt on later trials by gradually moving the correct colored object back so it's in line with the colored object. Continue to wait 3-5 seconds for a response and 3-5 seconds between trials. And be sure to switch the objects from side to side so the child will not learn a position habit.

Once the child is picking the correct color, ask the child to point to or hand you the other color. When the child can discriminate between the two colors, move to another color. Again, make it easy for the child. Red and green would be easier than red and yellow. Children with neuropsychological disorders may not generalize from one set of colors to another, so be prepared to spend a long time in discrete trial training. If you get no improvement after a large number of trials, try black and white discrimination because the child may be color-blind although color blindness is rare. After you have taught your child colors using DTT move on to shapes, then numbers and letters, followed by sight words. Your child will learn faster if you make DTT like a game--lots of reinforcement and plenty of breaks.

DTT apps:

DTT works even better on the iPhone, iPod touch, or the iPad. Caregivers, therapists, and educators can easily learn to use these DTT Apps on the Phone, iPod touch, or iPad or iPhone and save thousands of dollars on therapy bills.

In our clinic, we test all of our apps on children with Autism, ADD, ADHD, and other childhood developmental disorders. Complete instructions are included within each app. Each of our DTT apps has a setup screen that allows you to enter the basic parameters such as correct and incorrect stimuli--colors, shapes, numbers, letters, or sight words, timing settings and number and type of cards to display. After you select the basic settings and press start, the app simply displays multiple stimulus cards on the screen and verbally announces to your child the name of the correct stimulus that should be touched. After your child has touched a one of the stimuli, the app gives positive verbal feedback to your child, letting them know if they pressed the correct or incorrect stimulus. After ten questions/trials the app will display the number of correct answers received, and it will also write a log entry so that these results can be reviewed later.

Maintenance and Generalization:

Continue to deliver social reinforcement in the form of praise, hugs, pats on the back, etc. as often as you can once the child learns the difference between stimuli. Edible reinforcers, such as candy or other treats, may be faded out once a significant change from baseline is achieved. Only give the tangible reinforcer every other time, then every third time, etc. until it is no longer required to maintain appropriate behavior. Of course, social reinforcement should be given as often as possible.

If you are not getting anywhere after several weeks, contact a psychologist versed in ABA in your area if at all possible. (Go to www.bacb.com to locate ABA therapists.) One possibility for the

ABA program not working is satiation. In other words, your child is getting tired of whatever reinforcer you are using.
See http://www.polyxo.com/discretetrial/ for a good overview of discrete trial training.

Additional App Info and Links:
Dr. Brown's apps for iOS: **http://drbrownsapps.com/apps/**
- Autism/DTT Colors
- Autism/DTT Shapes
- Autism/DTT Letters
- Autism/DTT Numbers
- DTT Words
- DTT People
- DTT Animals
- DTT Pro *(Contains all the apps above plus)*:
    - DTT Bully
    - DTT Nouns
    - DTT Time

Dr. Brown's Autism/DTT apps are also available on other platforms:
Dr. Brown's apps for Amazon Kindle: **http://goo.gl/ua1Dky**
- DTT Colors Full
- DTT Shapes

Video reviews for our apps and many more special needs apps can be found at: www.drBrownsApps.com

Program 11: **Establishing Verbal Behavior in Children**

Children with neuropsychological disorders often have language delays for one reason or another. Since language is functional, children with language delays frequently resort to aggressive behavior, tantrums, and self-injurious behavior in order to communicate. A speech language pathologist should evaluate your child; however, if your child is non-compliant, the evaluation may not get very far. The speech language pathologist may suggest teaching your child sign language or a picture communication system. Do not be alarmed. Both of these procedures teach the child that he or she must do something to communicate. The research shows that teaching a nonverbal child sign language or a picture exchange system increases the likelihood that spoken language will develop.

Normally, children learn language by watching and imitating parents and siblings in the home and teachers and peers at daycare. It is very important to expose your child to conversation in the home. Be sure that the family talks frequently and uses language to communicate their needs instead of pointing and gesturing.

There is the old joke about the 8-year-old who blurted out, "This soup is too hot," at the table. The parents were amazed. "We've never heard you say anything before," they said to him. "Well, up to now everything has been okay." Not that funny, but it illustrates that language has a purpose.

The procedure below teaches the child the functionality of language and that may be all that is necessary to get the nonverbal child talking.

Behavioral Assessment

Count the number of functional words your child uses each day over a five- to seven-day period. A functional word is a word used to get the child something he or she wants or a verbal response to a verbal question or statement from someone else. For example, if a child is thirsty and says, "drink," that is a functional word. If a child responds correctly to a yes or no question from someone, that is functional as well. Words that are babbled while the child plays are not functional words.

Also note how your child communicates. Does he/she point at something to get what he/she wants? Growl or scream? Or does your child not need to communicate? Many times speech does not develop simply because parents anticipate and take care of their child's needs ahead of time. I have seen more than one mother refill her child's sippy cup before it is half empty. With "service" like that, who needs to talk?

Behavioral Intervention

Whenever your child does speak, makes an attempt to speak, makes a sound, or even moves his/her lips, say "I sure like the way you are talking," or "I sure like the way you are trying to talk." Rub his or her cheek, hug your child, pat him or her on the back, give chips, candy, cookies, or whatever else your child enjoys. (A Tupperware bowl full of bite size goodies is what we use as tangible reinforcers for most kids in our clinic. The child only gets to pick one bite size piece.) Of course, respond immediately to your child's verbal request or attempt at a verbal request.

Require speech, or at least an approximation of speech, such as a sound, for all communication. Do not anticipate your child's needs, but make your child communicate. Do not respond if your child tries to pull you towards what he or she wants or respond to pointing, but require some sound. Then, after he or she makes a sound, respond the same way you did above.

Do not talk for your child or try to coax your child to speak. Continue to keep a count of the number of functional words your child uses each day.

Everyone needs to follow this program. Once the child is consistently using single words to communicate, require two or three word phrases. For example, "I want drink."

If there is not a significant change from baseline after two weeks, contact a psychologist versed in ABA in your area if at all possible. (Go to www.bacb.com to locate ABA therapists.) One possibility for the ABA program not working is satiation. In other words, your child is getting tired of whatever reinforcer you are using. Try something different. And be sure everyone is following the ABA program and requiring at least a sound for the child to get what he or she wants.

Maintenance and Generalization

As always, continue to deliver social reinforcement in the form of praise, hugs, pats on the back, etc. as often as you can following appropriate behavior. Edible reinforcers, such as candy or other treats, may be faded out once a significant change from baseline is achieved. Only give the edible reinforcer every other time, then every third time, etc. until it is no longer required to maintain appropriate behavior. Of course, social reinforcement should be given as often as possible and always respond to the verbal request or attempt at a verbal request immediately where appropriate.

Please use the following form:

aba_p11_verbal.pdf- http://files.drbrownsapps.com/

Bonus Program: Increasing Verbal Behavior in Children

As I mentioned in ABA Procedure Number 11, children with neuropsychological disorders often have language delays for one reason or another. Since language is functional, children with language delays frequently resort to aggressive behavior, tantrums, and self-injurious behavior in order to communicate.

Normally, children learn language by watching and imitating parents and siblings in the home and teachers and peers at daycare. It is very important to expose your child to conversation in the home. Be sure that the family talks frequently and uses language to communicate their needs instead of pointing and gesturing.

The procedure below should be used along with: 11. Applied Behavioral Analysis (ABA) Procedure for Establishing Verbal Behavior in Children. The drills below are designed to increase the child's opportunity to use language.

Behavioral Assessment

Have ten pictures or objects on hand that your child knows the names of. Show the child the pictures or objects and record whether or not the child names the picture or object correctly. Only say, "What's this?" one time and do not plead or beg the child to answer. Run this drill several times a day for several days and that should provide an adequate baseline.

Behavioral Intervention

Show your child the ten pictures or objects again, saying, "What's this?" one time. Have some reinforcer in your hand that you know your child likes. Whenever your child answers correctly, praise the child and immediately give the reinforcer. Do not plead or beg the child to answer.

If there is not a significant change from baseline after several days, try another reinforcer. Once the child is able to name all ten pictures or objects, repeat the procedure with ten more pictures or objects and repeat again.

Maintenance and Generalization

Always deliver social reinforcement in the form of praise, following appropriate behavior. Edible reinforcers, such as candy or other treats, may be faded out once a significant change from baseline is achieved. Only give the edible reinforcer every other time, then every third time, etc. until it is no longer required to maintain appropriate behavior. Of course, social reinforcement should be given as often as possible and always respond to the verbal request or attempt at a verbal request immediately where appropriate.

Please use the following form:

aba_p11b_verbal.pdf- http://files.drbrownsapps.com/

Program 12: Eliminating Chewing on Objects and Pica

Many children with neuropsychological disorders constantly chew on toys, clothing, furniture, themselves, and occasionally, others. In addition to chewing, kids with neuropsychological disorders may pick up inedible objects off the floor or ground and eat them. This is called pica. Excessive chewing and pica can occur together or separately. Usually, chewing and/or pica occur at very high rates. Often the child will have periods of excessive chewing and/or pica and then there will be periods of time when this behavior subsides and even disappears for a while. But it usually always comes back.

Behavioral Assessment

The assessment of excessive chewing and/or pica can be a little tricky. Since these behaviors can occur at such a high rate, it is often impossible to count them individually.

In these cases, time the periods when chewing and/or pica behavior does not occur over a one-hour period in order to get a sample for a baseline. Record these times each day on the attached form for five days and that should be a sufficient baseline. (If chewing and/or pica are occurring at a low enough rate, then go ahead and count them.)

Note the antecedents (what happens before the excessive chewing/pica) and the consequences of chewing and/or pica (what happens after). Sometimes a child will engage in these behaviors for attention. In other words, a parent gives the child attention whenever he or she chews on something or tries to eat some thing inedible. But often excessive chewing and/or pica is a compulsive behavior with no apparent environmental consequences.

Behavioral Intervention

Whenever you notice your child chewing on anything (this includes his hands, fingers, sucking his thumb, toys, you, etc.), then you should use the "no" command. Say the single word "no" and clap your hands together loudly when you say the word. Say the word loud enough for your child to hear, but do not shout. If your child stops chewing or trying to eat something inedible, then praise him or her and thank your child for minding. Occasionally, give your child a small edible reward such as a bite of candy, a sip of coke, or whatever else he or she enjoys. (A Tupperware bowl full of bite size goodies is what we use as tangible reinforcers for most kids in our clinic. The child only gets to pick one bite size piece.)

If the child does not stop chewing or trying to eat some inedible object, then clap your hands together again, say the word "no," and take whatever he or she is chewing on, or trying to eat, away. Then quickly take the child to the bathroom, and using a soft bristle toothbrush that has been soaking in mouth wash, put the toothbrush in the child's hand and have the child brush his or her teeth for one minute. After the child has brushed his or her teeth, have the child wash his or her lips, and clean up the wash area. Tell the child repeatedly why he or she has to do this. (This is called an overcorrection procedure.) Keep track of the number of times you use the overcorrection procedure.

If there is not a significant change from baseline after two weeks, contact a psychologist versed in ABA in your area, if at all possible. (Go to www.bacb.com to locate ABA therapists.)

Maintenance and Generalization

Continue to deliver social reinforcement in the form of praise, hugs, pats on the back, etc. as often as you can following appropriate behavior. Edible reinforcers, such as candy or other treats, may be faded out once a significant change from baseline is achieved. Only give the edible reinforcer every other time, then every third time, etc. until it is no longer required to maintain appropriate behavior. Of course, social reinforcement should be given as often as possible.

Please use the following form:

aba_p12_chewing.pdf- http://files.drbrownsapps.com/

Program 13: Teaching Children to Model Appropriate Behavior

Many children with neuropsychological disorders do not behave appropriately and acquire new developmental skills because they do not observe and imitate others. Once a child learns how to imitate the behavior of others, the total number of appropriate behaviors in which the child engages greatly increases.

Behavior Assessment

Say, "do this," and hold up your hand in front of the child. Many children will imitate this response or at least reach up for your hand. Engage in a number of other behaviors and keep a count of how many behaviors your child imitates. Do this for several days and always ask the child to imitate the same behaviors the same number of times. This is your baseline.

Behavioral Intervention

If your child imitates you, or reaches for your hand, praise the child and give a small edible reinforcer. If the child is reinforced adequately by praise, then that is fine. Start with behaviors the child is highly likely to imitate. For example, if you hold your hand up in front of a child's face as you say, "do this," the child is likely to imitate or at least reach for your hand. (A Tupperware bowl full of bite size goodies is what we use as tangible reinforcers for most kids in our clinic. The child only gets to pick one bite size piece.)

If your child refuses to imitate, then use a physical prompt. Take the child's hand and raise it for him after raising your hand and saying, "do this." Then praise the child. Wait 3-5 seconds and repeat the "do this" command with the physical prompt followed by reinforcement. Fade the physical prompt as quickly as you can. In other words, use less and less force to hold up your child's hand, then move your hand to the elbow and simply initiate the move. It should not take long to get the child to imitate you for reinforcement.

After the child is imitating without a prompt, then move on to another simple motor behavior. Start each session with behaviors the child can do and then move to a behavior the child cannot do that requires a physical prompt. Stick with simple one-step motor behaviors, "do this," until your child is imitating reliably and then move on to two-step motor behaviors, "do this and this." If your child is nonverbal, try adding a sound after the motor behaviors and you may be able to establish verbal imitations using this procedure.

If there is not a significant change from baseline after two weeks, contact a psychologist versed in ABA in your area, if at all possible. (Go to www.bacb.com to locate ABA therapists.) One possibility for the ABA program not working is satiation. In other words, your child is getting tired of whatever reinforcer you are using. Try something different. And be sure everyone is following the ABA program.

Maintenance and Generalization

As often as you can, following appropriate behavior, deliver social reinforcement in the form of praise, hugs, pats on the back, etc. Tangible reinforcers, such as candy or other treats, may be faded out once a significant change from baseline is achieved. Only give the tangible reinforcer every other time, then every third time, etc. until it is no longer required to maintain appropriate behavior. Of course, social reinforcement should be given as often as possible.

Please use the following form:

aba_p13_behavior.pdf - http://files.drbrownsapps.com/

Program 14: **Eliminating Separation Anxiety**

Separation anxiety ranges from the child who always cries when left at daycare to the child who clings to mom all day and will not venture several feet from her even at home. Not all children with neuropsychological disorders have separation anxiety. In fact, a lack of interest in social and physical contact is often a defining feature of neuropsychological disorders like autism. On the other hand, some children with neuropsychological disorders have extreme separation anxiety.

Behavioral Assessment

How you approach the assessment differs depending on the severity of the separation anxiety. For the child who cries at daycare, ask the staff to record how long the child cries after the parent leaves for four to five days or until the baseline is stable, i.e., not trending up or down. The antecedent conditions, such as who takes the child, time of day, what the child does in the morning before going to daycare (complains of a stomach-ache, cries, tantrums, etc.) should be noted. The staff's reaction to the crying child, as well as the other kids' reactions, should also be recorded. (Sometimes it is difficult to get an accurate assessment from day care staff. They want you to feel like they can handle your child. All you can do is talk with the staff and assure them that you want accurate information and that you will in no way think that they are incompetent.)

In the case of severe separation anxiety, when the mom cannot even put the child down, the assessment procedure is different. Mom should sit on the floor in the child's room with the child in her lap. If the child is holding a toy, fine. Mom should record approximately how many feet, if any, the child ventures away from her. Twenty- to thirty-minute periods per day for four to five days should give us a good baseline. Antecedents and consequences should be recorded.

Behavioral Intervention

The behavioral intervention for the child who cries when left at daycare is rather simple. First, remove all uncertainty for the child who understands speech. Tell the child the time you are taking him or her to daycare and the time you are picking him/her up. Tell the child if there is no crying, complaining, etc., before daycare or when you leave him/her, then there will be some special treat when you pick him/her up. (Watching a video when the child gets home or trips to the park can be used if you do not want to use edible reinforcers.)

Ignore the child's crying, complaining, etc. before school if it occurs. When you arrive at daycare, repeat the time that you will pick up the child as you take him/her in and tell the child that you love him or her. Speed is important. Get in and out as quickly as possible. Let the staff take off the child's coat and do not stay and try to comfort the child. Tell the staff not to comfort (reinforce) the child's crying after you leave, but to get the child involved in activities instead. When you pick the child up, ask the staff if the child cried and how long. Most kids quickly decrease the time they cry and the separation anxiety problem is usually resolved in a week or less.

The first goal in the case of the child with extreme separation anxiety is to shape independent play behavior. In other words, we want to teach the child to be content without close physical contact and continuous attention from mom. Sit on the floor with the child in your lap and several of the child's favorite toys positioned in front of the child, out of reach. The toys should not be too far away, but far enough away that the child has to get out of your lap in order to get them. Do not hug the child, but sit quietly and wait for the child to get the toys. No doubt the child will ask for the toys, or if the child is nonverbal, he/she will point at the toys and whine. Do not move. Make the child get the toy on his/her own.

When the child does finally get up and retrieve the toy, immediately hug the child and tell him or her how proud you are that he or she went and got the toy and is playing with the toy. Tell the child he's a big boy or she's a big girl playing by himself or herself. You cannot be too lavish. If there are siblings or another parent present, have them participate in the praise.

Once the child is comfortable retrieving toys several feet away, move the toys several more feet and repeat the procedure. Do not rush this process. There is a close relationship between the gradual process of reducing separation anxiety and ABA Program Number 8.

Desensitizing a Child to Loud Noises. See the ABA Mini Program on the Turtle Technique in Appendix 1.

Continue to increase the distance the child has to go to retrieve the toys and continue the praise. Do not ever force the child to separate from you, but shape independent play behavior instead.

Maintenance and Generalization

In the case of the child who cries at daycare, continue to deliver social reinforcement in the form of praise, hugs, pats on the back, etc. as often as you can following appropriate behavior. Edible reinforcers, such as candy or other treats, may be faded out once a significant change from baseline is achieved. Only give the tangible reinforcer every other time, then every third time, etc. until it is no longer required to maintain appropriate behavior. Of course, social reinforcement should be given as often as possible.

Once the child with severe separation anxiety is comfortable playing independently in his or her room, move to a different room and repeat the procedure. You should reach the point when the child's natural exploratory drive overrides any remaining separation anxiety and the child will venture away from you on his or her own.

In the case of mild or severe separation anxiety, there should be a significant change from baseline within two weeks. If not, contact a psychologist versed in ABA in your area, if at all possible. (Go to www.bacb.com to locate ABA therapists.)

Please use the following form:

aba_p14_separation.pdf - http://files.drbrownsapps.com/

Program 15: **Eliminating Attention Deficits**

Attention deficits with hyperactivity (ADHD) and attention deficits without hyperactivity (ADD) are overdiagnosed, and as a result overmedicated kids are zombied out in many classrooms. Children with various neuropsychological disorders frequently present with attention deficits and/or hyperactivity, along with their other problems. Volumes of material have been written on the use of special diets, vitamins, medications, and behavioral interventions to treat ADD and ADHD, but usually kids end up on drugs. The ABA procedure to help manage attention deficits will be covered below. The next ABA program deals with hyperactivity.

Behavioral Assessment

Even for professionals this is a confusing area to assess. Stop and think what your child does that makes you think he or she has an attention deficit. Does your child not make eye contact with you? Does your child not follow directions? If this is the case, then look back at the table of contents and find the appropriate program. Here we will set up a program for the child who cannot attend to the relevant aspects of the environment and maintain attention.

Another way of looking at this is the child who does not stay on task for a reasonable period of time. Children with autism or some other neuropsychological disorders may do the opposite. They perseverate. In other words, they repeat the same behavior over and over, fixated on a spinning toy, or they engage in some other repetitive behavior for long periods of time. At any rate, we are going to use a time measure for our baseline. How long a child looks at a video, plays with a certain toy, looks at a book, carries on a conversation, or does homework, would be good examples of behaviors to increase. Pick one of these behaviors, or if you have another particular adaptive behavior you want to increase in your child, that is fine. Time how long the child attends without getting distracted. It may take a week to get a stable baseline. Note what distracts the child (antecedents) and what happens when the child gets distracted (consequences).

Behavioral Intervention

Look at your baseline and get an idea of the average time your child attends to the specific activity you are trying to get him/her to engage in without getting distracted. For our example, let's say it is only 15 seconds. Since 15 seconds is an average, that means sometimes the child will attend for less than 15 seconds and sometimes more. The sometimes more is what we are interested in. Whenever the child attends for longer than 15 seconds, reinforce the child immediately and accompany the edible reinforcer with verbal praise that specifies that the reinforcement is being given for increased time on task. Give the child a short break and repeat. (A Tupperware bowl full of bite size goodies is what we use as tangible reinforcers for most kids in our clinic. The child only gets to pick one bite size piece.)

After a week or so, the average time the child attends to the task without being distracted should have increased. Now start reinforcing the child, using the procedure above, at the times that go beyond the new average. The time your child attends should increase, and after a week or less, you should have a new average to work with. Repeat this procedure until your child is attending to the task for a reasonable amount of time.

If there is not a significant change from baseline after two weeks, contact a psychologist versed in ABA in your area, if at all possible. (Go to www.bacb.com to locate ABA therapists.) One possibility for the ABA program not working is satiation. In other words, your child is getting tired of whatever reinforcer you are using. In some cases, medication may be needed. A pediatric neurologist should be consulted.

Maintenance and Generalization

Continue to deliver social reinforcement in the form of praise, hugs, pats on the back, etc., as often as you can following appropriate behavior. Edible reinforcers, such as candy or other treats, may be faded out once a significant change from baseline is achieved. Only give the edible reinforcer every other time, then every third time, etc. until it is no longer required to maintain appropriate behavior. Of course, social reinforcement should be given as often as possible. Also see the ABA Mini Program on Sitting Still in Appendix 1.

Please use the following form: aba_p15_adhd.pdf

Program 16: **Controlling Hyperactivity**

Activity levels in children vary widely. Although numerous rating scales for hyperactivity have been developed for parents and classroom teachers, deciding exactly what constitutes hyperactivity is still somewhat subjective.

Children with various neurological disorders may be hyperactive, running around the room, only occasionally stopping to inspect a toy or other object. Or they may be hypoactive, not interested in exploring the environment, perhaps rocking back and forth on the floor, or engaging in self-stimulatory behavior.

Behavioral Assessment

The neurological condition of the child may determine activity levels. When a child with hyperactivity comes to my clinic for the first time, I take him/her to the toy room and ask the parents to stay in the waiting room. Usually, the child sees all of the toys and gets excited. It is not unusual for the child to run around the room, exploring all of the different toys. I sit back and watch the child without saying anything, and often the child calms down on his own, sits down, and starts playing with one toy for an appropriate amount of time.

I then ask the parents to come into the playroom. If the child gets up when he sees them and becomes hyperactive after having calmed down, I know what is going to happen next. The parents will start telling the child not to run, slow down, etc., and the hyperactivity increases even more. (Sometimes the parents even chase the child around the room.) I know then, the child's hyperactivity has been conditioned by the parents' attention. On the other hand, if the child never calms down and the parents do not affect activity levels, then I know the child's hyperactivity is neurologically based.

The antecedent conditions (the parents) and the consequences (the attention) are obvious in the first example. The baseline should be a measure of how long the child is not being hyperactive.

Behavioral Intervention

When your child is hyperactive, do not say anything and do not chase the child. Asking him or her to slow down, sit still, etc. has no effect and will actually make the child more active. Wait until the child has stopped being hyperactive for approximately 10 seconds, and then praise him or her for sitting still, playing, or whatever other appropriate behavior the child is engaged in. Keep careful records of the periods of time the child is calm. Be sure to tell everyone who keeps your child to follow this program. (Edible reinforcers are not usually necessary since the attention from the parents and teachers is what is reinforcing the hyperactivity. However, if there is not a change from baseline, try edible reinforcers.)

This program takes time. There should be small increases from baseline in the frequency and length of time the child is not hyperactive. If there is no change from baseline after three weeks, contact a psychologist versed in ABA in your area, if at all possible. (Go to www.bacb.com to locate ABA therapists.)

Hyperactivity in some children is caused by a sleep disorder. Go to the table of contents and read the ABA program dealing with sleep disorders if the ABA program for hyperactivity is not working.

If your assessment determines that the child's hyperactivity is not related to the presence of parents or teachers and that talking has no effect on the hyperactivity, then medication will probably be necessary. A pediatric neurologist should be consulted.

Maintenance and Generalization

If you are using edible reinforcement, such as candy or other treats, they may be faded out once a significant change from baseline is achieved. Only give the edible reinforcer every other time, then every third time, etc. until it is no longer required to maintain appropriate behavior. Of course, social reinforcement in the form of praise should be given as often as possible.

The ABA Mini Program on Teaching a Child to Sit Still found in Appendix 1 may also be helpful.

Please use the following form:

aba_p16_hyper.pdf - http://files.drbrownsapps.com/

Program 17: Shaping Independent Play

Children with neuropsychological disorders often have problems planning their activities and engaging in activities that should be fun. These kids have short attention spans and are constantly asking caregivers for help in directing their play activities, sometimes minute by minute. Whining, repeating questions, nagging, self-stimulation, and constantly following the caregivers around quickly create an unpleasant situation. Performance deficits, deliberately giving the wrong answers to increase the amount of time and attention the child gets from the caregiver, are also common.

Behavioral Assessment

Make a list of 5 or 6 activities the child will already engage in for short periods of time without being distracted. (Do not worry if the periods of time the child will stay on the activities are very short.) These could be activities like coloring, watching a video, playing a game, doing a computer drill, or working a puzzle. Then take one of these activities and time how long the child stays on task with this activity. Repeat this procedure for all of the activities you have picked. Then later in the daytime how long the child engages in these activities again.

At the end of Day One, you should have two time measures on each activity. Take these baseline measures for 3-4 days. We should then have good baselines for comparison. Of course, note antecedent conditions (for example, parts of the activity are too difficult and the child gets frustrated) and consequences (some one helps the child out) as always.

Behavioral Intervention

Our goal is to slowly increase the amount of time the child spends on each activity to the point that the child will learn to enjoy the activity and play independently. We are going to increase the time by reinforcing the child for longer and longer periods of independent play with a "social" activity.

Pick one of the activities you have baseline measures on. For example, tell the child if he or she will color for ____, (and add a minute to what the child was doing during baseline), you will take the child outside for ten minutes, play a game, or engage in any other activity with the child that you know the child likes. Use an egg timer to time the activity. Repeat this procedure for all of the 4-5 activities for which you have assessment measures. Increased time for the last activity should lead to a more special reward for the child if possible.

The next day, add a minute to the required times and repeat the procedure. If the child cannot engage in the activity for an entire minute, just add 30 seconds. Go slowly and adapt the time intervals to the child.

Do not be unreasonable. Increase the time the child stays on task to a reasonable amount and stop. Usually, children are not going to color for hours. Add other activities as soon as the child is spending a reasonable amount of time on the 4-5 activities you have already chosen.

This procedure takes time, but eventually, you will have a child that can entertain himself/herself and with an increased attention span can learn more. Obviously, increasing the amount of time a child stays on task is important for school activities as well.

Maintenance and Generalization

Continue to deliver reinforcement in the form of "social" activities with you until you have a stable change from baseline. Social reinforcement may then be faded out by giving the social reinforcer every other time, then every third time, etc. until the social reinforcement is no longer required to maintain independent play behavior. Note: There is some similarity in the ABA programs for staying on task, elimination of separation anxiety, and shaping independent play behavior. The difference is in terms of what is maintaining the behavior, so choose carefully.

If there is not a significant change from baseline after two weeks, contact a psychologist versed in ABA in your area, if at all possible. (Go to www.bacb.com to locate ABA therapists.) Sometimes medication needs to be added to this ABA procedure. Consult a pediatric neurologist or a pediatrician experienced in prescribing these medications.

Please use the following form: aba_p17_play.pdf

Program 18: Eliminating Self-Stimulatory Behavior

Stereotypy or self-stimulatory behaviors are non-functional, repetitive motor or sensory behaviors. Self-stimulatory behaviors are found in many kids with developmental disabilities and various neuropsychological disorders, but children with autism are the most likely to exhibit self-stimulatory behaviors.

All of the sensory systems may be involved or a particular child may only self-stim in one sensory modality. Examples of self-stim in the visual system are repetitive blinking, hand-flapping, moving fingers in front of the eyes, staring at light, or gazing at other objects. Tapping the ears, snapping fingers, and making repetitive vocal sounds, such as "eeee," are examples of self-stim in the auditory system.

Tactile self-stim includes rubbing or scratching the skin, sometimes until it bleeds. Repetitive rocking stimulates the vestibular system (inner ear), licking and placing objects in the mouth stimulate taste, and repetitively smelling objects and people stimulates the olfactory system. Theoretically, self-stim maintains optimal arousal in a dysfunctional nervous system.

Behavioral Assessment

The assessment depends on the particular self-stim behavior that is occurring. The frequency of hand flapping, the number of objects smelled or licked, or the number of times the child makes an inappropriate vocal sound may be appropriate for a baseline. In other types of self-stim, how long lights are stared at, how long the child rubs his skin or scratches, or how long the child rocks back and forth may be good baseline measures. Note antecedent conditions, such as boredom, anxiety or fear, too much or too little stimulation in the environment, novel environments, etc., and consequences, such as attention. (Since self-stim behavior is usually reinforced internally; there are no environmental consequences.)

Behavioral Intervention

An ABA procedure called overcorrection is most generally used to eliminate self-stimulatory behavior. In this procedure, clap your hands together loudly and tell the child "no" in a firm tone whenever he or she self-stims. Then the child is told or made to practice a correct or incompatible behavior to the self-stim behavior. The goal is to "overcorrect" the environmental effects of the inappropriate behavior and require the child to "overly" practice appropriate behavior.

The exact overcorrection procedure used depends on the sensory system affected. For licking and placing objects in the mouth, the child is told "no" in a firm voice. Then quickly take the child to the bathroom, and using a soft bristle toothbrush that has been soaking in mouth wash, put the toothbrush in the child's hand. Have the child brush his or her teeth for one minute. After the child has brushed his or her teeth, have the child wash his or her lips, and clean up the wash area. Tell the child repeatedly why he or she has to do this. (The same procedure is used for pica in ABA Number 12.)

The overcorrection procedure for hand flapping is to tell the child "no" and then hold the child's hands stationary for thirty seconds. For head weaving, the head is held stationary for thirty seconds after the child is told "no."

The behavior that is "overly" practiced following "no" does not seem to really matter just as long as it is in the same sensory system and appropriate. So if a child is saying "eeee," have the child say words he or she knows after being told "no."

If there is not a significant change from baseline after two weeks, contact a psychologist versed in ABA in your area, if at all possible. (Go to www.bacb.com to locate ABA therapists.)

Maintenance and Generalization

Most of the research finds that not only are specific self-stim behaviors suppressed, but other types of untreated self-stim are also suppressed. Adaptive behavior, such as playing with toys, also increases. If self-stim behavior reappears, then initiate the overcorrection procedure again.

Drugs are often used to help eliminate self-stim behaviors. Dosage and drug choice are crucial because the goal is not to interfere with overall motor functioning and have a sedated child. Consult a pediatric neurologist or a pediatrician experienced in the use of these drugs. Combining drug treatments with overcorrection often works well.

Please use the following form:

aba_p18_self.pdf - http://files.drbrownsapps.com/

Program 19: Eliminating Echolalia

Echolalia is the repetition or echoing of what another person says. Kids with autism are the most likely to engage in echolalia. Echoing songs the child heard on the radio or repeating TV commercials after a period of time has passed is called delayed echolalia

Immediate echolalia is the parroting of what was just said. The question, "Do you want some juice?" would be repeated by the child with autism rather than giving the correct answer. Repeating the question to the child again and again usually results in the same echo response and is very frustrating for caregivers and teachers.

Behavioral Assessment

Make a list of simple questions that you know your child can answer correctly. I usually start with a series of questions like, "What is your name? How are you doing? How old are you? What town do you live in?" etc. Ask the child each question orally, and for the baseline record whether or not the child echoes the question, even if the child gives the right answer after echoing the question. (As I discussed in the assessment section of the Overview of ABA, it is easier to calculate percentages if you always use groups of 10.) Generally, echolalia occurs at a stable rate, so asking the series of questions several times for 1 or 2 days will probably give us a stable baseline.

Behavioral Intervention

Since kids with autism are the most likely to engage in echolalia, it makes sense to take advantage of their special learning style. Auditory comprehension is almost always a problem in these kids, but visual processing is close to normal, maybe even advanced, in children with autism. I learned many years ago to use visual cues.

Write one or two word answers to the list of questions you used for the baseline on 3 x 5 index cards. (Sometimes pictures can be used as answers rather than printed answers.)

Ask the child each question like you did in the assessment phase except this time quickly hold up the 3 x 5 card so the child can read the correct answer before he or she has a chance to echo the question. If necessary, verbally prompt the child with the correct answer if the child cannot recognize what is on the card.

Praise the child whenever he or she answers correctly without echolalia. As soon as the child stops echoing to the list you have prepared, add more questions. It is also appropriate at this point to add some questions the child does not know the answer to and prompt the child to say, "I do not know." After the child can answer "I do not know" correctly, write down the correct answer to the question and prompt the child if necessary.

If there is not a significant change from baseline after two weeks, contact a psychologist versed in ABA in your area, if at all possible. (Go to www.bacb.com to locate ABA therapists.)

Maintenance and Generalization

The social reinforcement (the praise) may be faded out once a significant change from baseline is achieved. Only praise every other time, then every third time, etc. until praise is no longer required to maintain appropriate behavior.

Please use the following form:

aba_p19_echo.pdf - http://files.drbrownsapps.com/

Program 20: **Eliminating Repetitive Vomiting**

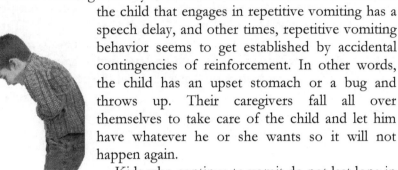

All kids vomit at one time or another. But some kids learn that repetitive vomiting is a way to control their environment. Sometimes the child that engages in repetitive vomiting has a speech delay, and other times, repetitive vomiting behavior seems to get established by accidental contingencies of reinforcement. In other words, the child has an upset stomach or a bug and throws up. Their caregivers fall all over themselves to take care of the child and let him have whatever he or she wants so it will not happen again.

Kids who continue to vomit do not last long in daycare, preschool, or even school.

Be sure to consult your pediatrician about your child's repetitive vomiting before you begin this ABA program.

Behavioral Assessment

I doubt that any parent will have difficulty counting the number of times their child throws up. The number of times the child throws up each day will be our baseline.

Antecedent conditions are usually the child getting frustrated, being given a direction that he or she does not want to follow, separation anxiety, a fear or phobia, or boredom. Some kids stick their fingers down their throats to make themselves throw up, but this is not really an antecedent condition as far as ABA is concerned. Of course, the consequences are the child immediately gets control of the situation, and more than likely, tender loving care.

Behavioral Intervention

The child has to learn that repetitive vomiting is not going to control people any more. Unfortunately, this behavioral intervention is not going to be pretty. Stock up on a good supply of plastic drop cloths from the paint store so clean-up will be easier. Place a drop cloth or two on the floor of the room where the child spends most of his or her time and cover beds and furniture if necessary. The doors to other rooms of the house should be kept closed.

Determine from your assessment what the antecedents to

vomiting are in your child. For example, let's say it is being given a direction. Then take the child into the room where the drop cloths are located and give the child one direction after another. If the child throws up, then leave the room and shut the door. (A peephole can be installed in the door--reversed so you can see in.) The room is like time out with a mess.

After the child has stopped throwing up for five minutes, go back in the room, and repeat the direction that caused the vomiting. If the child follows the direction without throwing up, praise him or her and give him/her a nonedible reinforcer. If the child throws up, then leave the room again and do not come back until five minutes after the last vomiting episode. Repeat the direction again and either reinforce the child for not vomiting and following the direction or leave again.

After you have reinforced the child, wait five minutes and have the child help you clean up the drop cloths. Put the drop cloths in plastic bags and clean up your child. Tell the child the procedure will be repeated every time he or she vomits. During this phase of the program, it is best to keep the child at home.

It the child vomits at mealtime, terminate the meal and put the child in the room with the drop cloths. Repeat the above procedure and the child gets no more food until the next meal. At the next meal, only give half the amount of food that you normally give the child. Let the child finish that amount, and if the child indicates he or she wants more and has made no attempt to throw up, give a little more. Praise the child for not throwing up during mealtime.

If there is not a significant change from baseline after two weeks, contact a psychologist versed in ABA in your area, if at all possible. (Go to www.bacb.com to locate ABA therapists.)

Maintenance and Generalization

Continue to deliver social reinforcement in the form of praise, hugs, or pats on the back when the child follows directions consistently and does not vomit. Nonedible reinforcers may be faded out once a significant change from baseline is achieved. Only give the reinforcer every other time, then every third time, etc. until it is no longer required to maintain appropriate behavior. Of course, social reinforcement should still be given as often as possible.

Please use the following form: aba_p20_vomit.pdf

Program 21: **Increasing Social Behavior**

Social problems are common in kids with neuropsychological disorders such as autism. Many think that difficulties with social behavior are the defining feature of autism and other pervasive developmental disorders. Some kids with autism avoid people altogether and run away, tantrum, engage in self-injurious behavior, or become aggressive if someone attempts to interact with them.

Other kids with autism or other neuropsychological disorders are simply indifferent to people in their environment and treat them like pieces of furniture. They do not get upset if someone interacts with them, but they get no pleasure from the interaction.

Higher functioning kids with autism, Asperger Syndrome, or other neuropsychological disorders are usually socially awkward. These kids want to interact and have friends, but they do not engage in appropriate conversation, and are often self-centered and talk only about themselves or perseverate on other topics.

Behavioral Assessment

Kids who run from social interactions and/or tantrum or engage in other inappropriate behavior are often hyperreactive to sensory stimuli. Noise, touch, and other sensory stimuli are aversive and sometimes painful. This is usually easy to pick up on in the assessment. Note the antecedent conditions of the child's inappropriate behaviors and see if increases in touch, noise, or other stimuli are involved. Sometimes these children will even cover their ears.

If your assessment determines that your child is hyperactive to sensory stimuli, you need to also read ABA Program Number 8, Desensitization to Loud Noises. Desensitization to aversive or painful stimuli must occur before social behavior can improve. (If your child is hyperreactive to other types of sensory stimuli, the program should be adjusted. Start out with the sensory stimuli at a low level and use something the child finds pleasant to override the hyperreactivity. Then gradually increase the intensity and/or duration of the sensory stimuli.)

The child who is indifferent usually does not make eye contact with others (which is covered in ABA Program Number 1) or initiate or respond verbally. These kids need to increase the frequency of appropriate verbal interactions—it is usually zero--as does the socially awkward child who only talks about himself.

The number of appropriate verbal interactions over a set period of time is usually adequate for a baseline. Note antecedents, such as to whom the child is most likely to talk, if anyone. Often these kids are silent in social situations, especially with kids their own age.

Behavioral Intervention

A lot of research, as well as personal testimony from children and adults who have recovered from autism, suggests that kids with autism think in pictures. In our clinic, we take a series of pictures to use as visual prompts and put them in a notebook with writing above them much like a comic strip in the newspaper.

The first picture in the series should be of the caregiver and the child. The caption should read, "(Child's name), if you go and say hi to (name a kid), I will give you (name the reinforcer)." The second picture should be of your child walking over to the designated child. The third picture should be your child saying hi to the designated child, and the last picture should be of the caregiver giving the child the reinforcer and telling the child what it is for. (A Tupperware bowl full of bite size goodies is what we use as tangible reinforcers for most kids in our clinic. The child only gets to pick one bite size piece.)

After you have the series of pictures, the caregiver should sit down with the child away from the designated child. The caregiver should read the captions and show the child each picture. Then the caregiver should verbally prompt the child to approach the designated child and say "hi," reminding the child of the reinforcer he or she gets afterward. If necessary, take the child's hand and walk him or her over to the child the first few times. Then after the child says "hi," deliver the reinforcer and praise the child. Repeat this procedure every five to ten minutes for an hour in the morning and an hour in the afternoon. If the child spontaneously says "hi" to another child, then reinforcement should be delivered. Do not worry if the child cannot read or has a limited vocabulary.

As soon as the child is saying "hi" reliably, require that the child add the designated child's name in order to get the reinforcer. Change the caption in the appropriate picture and add more words as the child learns the new greeting.

This same procedure can also be used for the child who is socially awkward and makes inappropriate responses or engages in self-centered conversation. The captions on the pictures should contain appropriate conversation.

Maintenance and Generalization

As often as you can, once you have a noticeable change from baseline that is stable, deliver social reinforcement in the form of praise, hugs, or pats on the back following socially appropriate verbal behavior. If you are using edible reinforcers, such as candy or other treats, they may be faded out once a significant change from baseline is achieved. Only give the tangible reinforcer every other time, then every third time, etc. until it is no longer required to maintain appropriate behavior. Of course, social reinforcement should still be given as often as possible.

The visual prompts can also be faded once there is a significant change from baseline. Hold the pictures up for the child without reading the captions and then point to the designated child. Next only hold up the picture of the child interacting and the child getting reinforced. Then hold up the last picture only. Most kids will have the drill down by this time and are making socially appropriate verbal interactions spontaneously. The ABA Mini Program on Teaching a Child to Share found in Appendix 1 is also useful. Social stories can also convey information on how to behave in social situations.

Please use the following form:

aba_p21_social.pdf - http://files.drbrownsapps.com/

Program 22: **Teaching Children to Listen and Remember Directions**

Many children who come to our clinic, some with and some without neuropsychological disorders, do not listen to directions. Or if they listen, they do not remember the directions for a very long period of time and make mistakes. Delays and/or distractions contribute greatly to this problem, as do parents and other caregivers who constantly remind the child of what he/she should do next. And processing auditory information can be difficult for children with autism and related disorders. (Of course some children are noncompliant and do not follow directions at all. If this is the case, the first ABA program in this volume for Following Directions should be used for these children.)

Behavioral Assessment

In the assessment, we want to first determine how long the child can remember a one-step direction. Tell your child that you are going to give him/her a direction, and tell your child that he/she is going to have to wait 5 seconds before following the direction. Then give the child a one step-direction that you know the child can do and count silently to 5. Next tell the child, "Now do what I asked you to do." Repeat this step with different one-step directions using a 5-second delay. If the child performs/remembers the directions with a 5-second delay, then increase the delay to 20 seconds and repeat the drill. Continue to increase the delay by 10 seconds until you find that the child has a problem remembering. There is probably no need in going beyond 5 minutes. If your child cannot remember simple one-step directions for longer than 5 minutes, then follow the behavioral intervention below for increasing delays.

If you find that your child has no problem remembering one-step directions, then proceed on to two-step directions with a 5-second delay. Again, vary the directions and increase the delay interval by 10 seconds until you find the child's limit. Keep good records on the form provided of successes and failures and the delay intervals where they occur.

Behavioral Intervention

The behavioral intervention should be treated like a game. Fill a Tuper-Ware bowl full of goodies such as skittles, M&M's, goldfish, chips, etc.--anything your child likes, or if you do not want to use candy, have a supply of stickers on the table.

To increase the length of time your child remembers a one-step direction, start at the time delay where errors were occurring in the assessment. Tell your child if he/she remembers to follow the direction, then a _____ will be given as a prize. Cue the child to repeat the direction over and over in his/her head. Then give the one-step direction and reward successful behavior with praise and candy or a sticker. Do not get upset or show your disappoint over errors. Simply say, "Let's play again." Continue to keep records of successes and failures like you did in the assessment. Mix it up--but stick with one-step directions and gradually increase the time intervals as the child is successful. Always cue the child each time to repeat the direction but do not nag the child to pay attention. When the child is able to remember one-step directions for 5 minutes, move on to two-step directions. This may take a few minutes, a few days, a few weeks, or a few months.

Repeat the above procedure for two-step directions, gradually increasing the delay until you get the child to the point that he/she can remember two-step directions for 5 minutes. Always use simple directions that you know the child can follow. If age appropriate, use paper and pen exercises, such as circle certain letters in a coloring book, etc; and simulate school activities. For older children it would be appropriate to repeat the procedure for three-step directions.

Maintenance and Generalization

Deliver social reinforcement in the form of praise, hugs, or pats on the back following successful behavior. If you are using edible reinforcers, such as candy or other treats, they may be faded out. Only give the tangible reinforcer every other time, then every third time, etc. until it is no longer required for maintaining appropriate behavior. Of course, social reinforcement should still be given as often as possible following successful behavior.

The ABA Mini Program for teaching a child to hurry up also goes well with this program.

Please use the following form: aba_p22_listen.pdf

Program 23: **Reducing Frustration in Children**

Children, with or without neuropsychological disorders, become frustrated when they do not get their way or they are faced with tasks they cannot do. And nonverbal children especially become frustrated over not being able to communicate their wants and needs.

Frustration may lead to a variety of behavioral problems including tantrums, aggressive behavior, or self-injurious behavior. At the very least, frustration interferes with learning appropriate behavior efficiently, so it must be dealt with if the child is going to overcome his or her developmental delays.

If the ABA programs for decreasing tantrums, aggressive behavior, self-injurious behavior, or other problem behaviors, do not completely eliminate the behavior, but only decrease it, then you need to teach your child how to handle frustration.

Behavioral Assessment

Note the antecedent conditions. What leads to frustration in your child? This may be obvious, but list the antecedent conditions anyway. The consequences should be obvious also. The behavior that follows prolonged frustration, tantrums, aggressive behavior, or other inappropriate behavior, is going to be reinforced by caregivers and/or get the child out of the frustrating situation.

The baseline is going to be a little complicated. With most children, frustration is like water boiling in a pot. Unless the heat is turned down, the water is going to boil over. Similarly, unless something is done to decrease the child's frustration, inappropriate behavior is going to occur. For the baseline, try to time the interval between the antecedent conditions that trigger frustration and the appearance of inappropriate behavior. (The interval may be very short, too short to time with a watch. If this is the case, simply count the interval in your head and write it down. You may find that the interval varies with different antecedent conditions, whether or not the child is tired, and so on. So keep a record of the time intervals for the different antecedent conditions and the child's condition.)

Behavioral Intervention

Once you have a stable baseline, not trending up or down, of the time intervals between the antecedent conditions that trigger frustration and the inappropriate behavior that results, you can begin the intervention. What we want to do is to set up "drills" to teach the child an alternative response to frustration. The alternate response depends on the cognitive level of the child. For some children, learning a verbal or non-verbal signal that he or she is getting frustrated and needs help is effective. The verbal child can be taught to say, "Help me please," while the non-verbal child can be shown how to sign for help. (The sign for help is: 1. Raise your left hand. With your right hand make a fist with your thumb over-lapping your fingers. 2. Hold your left hand out in front of you with your palm up and flat. 3. Rest your right hand in a fist on the palm of your left hand. 4. Then with a small up-sweeping motion raise together your left and right hand.)

For higher functioning children, teaching a relaxation response, such as the Turtle Technique, found in Appendix 1, is a good way to handle frustration. In the "turtle technique" whenever the child starts to feel frustration, he/she is to put his/her hands over his/her head and pretend that he/she is a turtle in a warm, cozy shell where he/she can relax. The child can be cued to take a deep breath and relax until he/she feels calm again. Then the child can put his/her hands down and come out of the shell. This is a self-management technique, but in the beginning we will have to cue the child to do this on his/her own. Stickers can be given to the child each time he/she uses the turtle technique to manage frustration.

Whichever alternative response is taught to the child, drills using the antecedent conditions that trigger frustration should be set up to allow for extensive practice. Continue to keep careful records of the time interval between the antecedent conditions and the occurrence of the inappropriate behavior.

Maintenance and Generalization

Only give the tangible reinforcer every other time, then every third time, etc. until it is no longer required for maintaining appropriate behavior. Continue to deliver social reinforcement in the form of praise, hugs, or pats on the back following successful behavior. Of course, social reinforcement should still be given as often as possible following successful behavior.

Please use the following form: aba_p23_frustration.pdf

Program 24: Sleep Cycle Problems

Children with autism, ADHD, and other neuropsychological disorders frequently have sleep problems. Some of these sleep problems are associated with their syndromes, while others are a side effect of the medications used to treat the various neuropsychological disorders. Thirty percent of parents report some problems in getting their kids to go to bed alone and often, problems in getting them to sleep throughout the night.

Many of these problems are minor, but in addition to sleep problems associated with various neuropsychological disorders and medication, children can also suffer from the same sleep disorders as adults. Insomnia, narcolepsy, restless leg syndrome, sleep apnea type disorders (enlarged tonsils/ adenoids are causing loud snoring or gasping for air), night terrors, sleep walking, and delayed sleep phase syndrome are all found in children.

Behavioral Assessment

Assessment of certain sleep problems can be difficult even in a sleep clinic. Sleep studies require an overnight stay of twelve hours and there is a shortage of certified pediatric sleep clinics. And of course, you may have to battle your insurance company in order to get coverage. Ask your child's pediatrician if he or she thinks a sleep clinic is the best way to go.

A pediatrician should also be able to tell you if your child's sleep problems are behavioral or associated with the child's disorder, medication being used to treat the disorder, or some other medical problem. For example, medications such as the SSRI's, which are used to treat autism, can interfere with sleep and the pediatric neurologist may prescribe a drug like clonodine to help the child sleep.

If the sleep disorder has a behavioral component, keep a diary of your child's sleep patterns for a week. Write down the time of day the child naps and for how long. Do the same thing at night. Note the antecedent conditions--what happens before the child sleeps and after. Also note what happens at bedtime. What do you do to try and get your child to bed and to stay in bed and what do you do if your child wakes up during the night? And also note where the child sleeps.

Behavioral Intervention

For the child who will not sleep alone in his or her own bed:
1. Do not let your child have caffeine.
2. Put your child's mattress on the floor in your room by your bed.
3. Tell your child that he or she is a big boy or girl and from now on he/she will be sleeping in his/her own bed. Tell your child other kids his or her age do not sleep in their parents' bed, and that for now, the mattress will be beside your bed but each night it will be moved three feet until it is in the child's room.
4. Also tell your child that if he/she sleeps on the mattress without complaining, getting up, etc., he or she will receive _____ as reinforcement in the morning. However, each time he or she complains, gets up, refuses to stay in bed, or engages in other inappropriate behavior, he/she will go to time out.
5. You and your spouse are to sleep in your own bed and go to bed at the time you wish.
6. Keep good records of your child's progress.

For the child who has difficulty going to sleep at night:
As I discussed in Case History Number 7, babies need to learn to fall asleep on their own. Do not rock them to sleep or feed them until they fall asleep. Put them in their cribs awake. It may take 20-30 minutes of crying for the baby to go to sleep, but this will not hurt the baby. (The crying is difficult for some moms so I often recommend Walkmans with their favorite music cranked up loud enough to partially mask the baby's crying.) Ninety percent of babies are sleeping through the night by the time they are three months old if this procedure is followed.

This procedure works, but requires self-discipline on the part of the parents. Other, less effective procedures let the parents off easier, at least for the short term. The approach of popular media pediatrician, Dr. Bob Sears, stops the baby's crying by letting the parents take the baby into their bed where it sleeps for the rest of the night. (And the odds are overwhelming that the baby will sleep there the next night and the next night.) Of course, the toll this takes on the parents is obvious and at some point the baby still has to learn to sleep in it's own bed. I've had parents who have followed this procedure bring their children to my clinic who are various ages (some not children anymore, but teens) for help in getting them to sleep in their own beds.

Another media pediatrician, Dr. Richard Ferber, recommends letting the baby cry for longer and longer periods of time before going in until it finally falls asleep, but this approach (known as Ferberizing) takes much longer, and I think it prolongs the child's and the parents' agony.

If your child is older and never learned to fall asleep, then the procedure is going to be more difficult. Keep the child on a strict schedule. Teach the child the Turtle Technique. In the Turtle Technique the child can learn to relax and fall asleep. He or she is to put his/her hands over his/her head and pretend that he/she is a turtle in a warm cozy shell where he/she can relax. The child can be cued to take a deep breath and relax until he/she feels calm. Then the child can put his/her hands down and come out of the shell. This is a self-management technique, but in the beginning we will have to cue the child to do this on his/her own. Stickers can be given to the child each time he/she uses the turtle technique to fall asleep.

Other things that you can add to the above procedure are:
- A protein rich snack before bed.
- Keep the room at 65% so the child will need a blanket.
- White masking noise.
- A long warm shower or bath before bedtime.
- A lava lamp or slow moving computer screen saver.

For the child who doesn't fall asleep until late at night:

Some children get enough sleep, but they don't fall asleep until late at night, sleep well into the morning, and usually take naps late in the afternoon or early evening. These children are often chronically tired and their sleep pattern is out of phase with the day/night cycle.

With these kids, slowly shift their bedtime to an earlier time by 30-minute intervals. Do the same for their nap times. You can also teach these children the Turtle Technique so they will fall asleep sooner.

The trick here is to go slow. You may find that you need to spend a week or so every time you shift to a new time. The research shows that adults that move to a new shift at work take 6 weeks to adjust.

Maintenance and Generalization

Continue to deliver social reinforcement in the form of praise, hugs, or pats on the back, following socially appropriate sleep behavior, as often as you can once you have a noticeable change from baseline. If you are using edible reinforcers, such as candy or other treats, they may be faded out once a significant change from baseline is achieved. Only give the tangible reinforcer every other time, then every third time, etc. until it is no longer required to maintain appropriate behavior. Of course, social reinforcement should still be given as often as possible.

Please use the following form:

aba_p24_sleep.pdf - http://files.drbrownsapps.com/

Program 25: **The Child Who Says "No"**

As I mentioned in ABA Program Number 1, children with neuropsychological disorders need to be compliant and follow directions. Otherwise, it is impossible to determine accurately the child's level of functioning. If a child does not follow directions from teachers and other professionals, then it is often assumed that the child is incapable of doing what is asked because of the deficits associated with his/her neuropsychological disorder. Many children with neuropsychological disorders do not reach their full potential simply because they are non-compliant and do not follow directions.

If your child is not already following directions at least half the time, run ABA Program One for increasing the number of directions followed by the child. This ABA program is for the verbal child who is usually compliant and follows directions, but at times says "no" and refuses to follow the direction. (Some children say "no" but follow the direction anyway. Just saying "no" should be handled the same as not following the direction. See below.)

Behavioral Assessment

Each day, for five days, give your child a one-step direction every five minutes for one hour. The direction should be something you already know the child can do. Record the number of times your child says "no" and refuses to follow the direction. (When you say "no," that is a direction for the child to stop doing something and can be included as one of the directions.) After five days, we should have a stable count of the number of times the child says "no" and refuses to follow directions. This can be used as our baseline for comparison after we have given our behavioral intervention a chance to work. (If the child says "no," do not repeat the direction and give him/her a second chance.)

Behavioral Intervention

Day Six: Before you give the child a direction, first, say the child's name in a firm tone as you did in ABA Program Number 1. Then give the direction also in a firm tone. Be sure you have the child's attention. In this program, attention = eye contact with you. If the child does not respond and make eye contact with you, clap your hands loudly and then give the direction if the child makes eye contact. If the child still does not respond and make eye contact with you, gently take the child's chin and turn his or her face toward you. Only give the command once and never plead or beg with the child to comply. No matter what the child is doing he/she should <u>immediately</u> comply.

If your child immediately follows the direction without saying "no," praise him or her, clap, give a small piece of candy, a sip of coke or juice, whatever the child likes, and show your child that you appreciate his or her minding, not saying "no," and doing what you ask. Occasionally, do something even more special when directions are followed without a "no" response. (A Tupperware bowl full of bite size goodies is what we use as tangible reinforcers for most kids in our clinic. The child only gets to pick one bite size piece.)

Of course the child will not always comply and follow the direction without saying "no." Whenever this happens, do not say anything, but immediately go get the child, tell the child that he or she is going to time out for saying "no" and not following your direction, and put the child in time out. (Do not threaten time out to get the child to follow the direction or repeat the direction and give the child a second chance. This might work for a while, but then time out becomes less effective.)

Time out is an often used and misused procedure. If done properly, time out is a very effective, humane procedure. Find a place in your house where a time out chair, preferably a chair with arms and not a bench, can be left. The chair should face a blank wall and not be close to a window, shelves, glass, electrical outlets, or storage cabinets containing chemicals. Hallways and alcoves often work. Do not use bathrooms or closets. The time out chair should be close to the play area so the child can be placed in time out quickly. Think safety, especially for small children. (If the child is very young, then the baby bed will do, and no, the child will not develop an aversion to the baby bed and have sleep problems. An alternative time out procedure for a young toddler is to sit him/her down on the floor with his/her back to you and hold them there for thirty seconds. Do not talk to the child except to tell him or her at the beginning and end of time out why they are in time out.)

For young toddlers, you can just count to thirty in your head. For older children, use an egg timer and teach the child that he or she cannot get out of time out until the egg timer goes off. The child has to stay in time out for three minutes plus one minute of good behavior. In other words, the child has to be quiet and cannot be arguing, complaining, or tantruming for one full minute before he or she can get out of time out.

Do not be surprised if the child comes up with a whole bag of new inappropriate behaviors in order to get out of time out. Children have been known to gag, vomit, and one of my own children even hit herself in the face several times. Do not respond and thereby reinforce these new inappropriate behaviors or they will increase in their frequency. Only good behavior gets the child out of time out. (Initially, some children have to be held in time out. Gradually, decrease the restraint you have on the child and make sure he/she is sitting there quietly for one minute before he/she gets out. If the child is too large to safely hold in time out, then use a response cost procedure instead. In response cost something the child values is taken away temporarily. Examples include: watching TV, going outside, videos, the opportunity to play games with caregivers, favorite foods or beverages, a favorite toy, etc.)

In the beginning of this procedure, it is not unusual for a child to be in time out for fifteen to twenty minutes before he/she quiets down, and to go to time out as often as twenty times a day. After a few days, the child learns the requirements of the time out procedure and he/she gets out in the minimum four minutes. The number of times the child goes to time out each day also drops dramatically. (Record the frequency and length of time outs on the form provided and you will see the child's progress.)

When the child gets out of time out, remind your child in a firm tone of why he or she had to go to time out. Tell your child that he/she will have to go again if your directions are not followed immediately without saying "no." Do not be timid with your voice or body language. Note: The time out procedure above is repeated in many, but not all of the ABA programs in this volume. There has been much written about time out, but I have found that this is the most effective procedure for most kids.

<u>Everybody</u> who cares for the child has to follow this procedure. Try to concentrate on the positive part of the program and not just

the negative.

If there is not a significant change from baseline after two weeks, contact a psychologist in your area who is versed in ABA, if at all possible. (Go to www.bacb.com to locate ABA therapists.) One possibility for the ABA program not working is satiation. In other words, your child is getting tired of whatever reinforcer you are using. Try something different. And be sure everyone is following the ABA program.

Maintenance and Generalization

Continue to deliver social reinforcement in the form of praise, hugs, pats on the back, etc. as often as you can following appropriate behavior. Edible reinforcers, such as candy or other treats, may be faded out once a significant change from baseline is achieved. Only give the tangible reinforcer every other time, then every third time, etc. until it is no longer required to maintain appropriate behavior. Of course, social reinforcement should be given as often as possible. If your child tantrums, becomes aggressive, engages in self-injurious behavior, or any other misbehavior when given a direction, then combine the ABA programs for these behaviors with the ABA procedure for following directions.

Please use the following form:

aba_book/aba_p25_no.pdf - http://files.drbrownsapps.com/

CHAPTER 3 **MINI-PROGRAMS**

The following mini-programs will hopefully help you with some common problems.

Mini-Program 1: **Teaching Children to Share**

Many children have to be taught to share. Sit the child down on the floor with another child who will cooperate. Have several toys on the floor between the two children. Hand a preferred toy, one that you know the child who does not share likes, to the cooperative child and a toy that is not as much preferred to the child who will not share. If the child who will not share plays with the toy for even a few seconds and does not go after the preferred toy, praise him or her and give a sticker or some other reinforcer. If you see the child who will not share "eyeing" the toy the other child has, tell him to ask the other child if he or she can play with the preferred toy. If the child who will not share asks nicely, then have the other child give the child who will not share the toy and praise the child who will not share for asking and praise the other child for sharing. Give stickers or some other reinforcer to both children.

Once the child who is not sharing is asking on a regular basis for the toy, and

getting the toy, introduce a short delay. Have the other child say, "Just a minute,

I'm still playing with it." Praise the child who will not share for waiting and give a sticker

or some other reinforcer. If at any time the child who will not share grabs the toy or is aggressive, then it is time out using the procedure described in ABA. Count the number of times the child will not share "share" appropriately and the number of times the child goes to time out and we will know how we are progressing.

Mini-Program 2: **Teaching a Child to Sit Still**

This is always the hard one for children with a tendency toward hyperactivity. But children have to learn the "sit" command if they are going to go to day care and be able to go places with their caregivers.

Several times a day sit the child on a mat and repeat the word "sit" every ten seconds and motion with your finger toward his mat. Keep the child sitting as long as you can, then just before the child moves, reinforce him/her for sitting with an M&M or some other treat. Keep repeating the word "sit" and giving the reinforcer.

If the child is too fast and moves off the mat before you can give the reinforcement, place him/her back on the mat and repeat the word "sit." Then reinforce the child for sitting still on the mat. Gradually increase the time required for reinforcement and gradually move a few feet away from the child as you are doing this procedure. Eventually, you want to be able to control the child's sitting from across the room. Then fade the reinforcer and only use praise to get the child to sit still.

Mini-Program 3: **Relaxing a Child Who is Upset**

Many children get upset and have trouble controlling their emotions. There are several techniques available to calm the child down and teach him or her to control his or her emotions in the future.

Whenever your child starts to get upset, you can teach him or her the "turtle technique." The child is cued to put his/her hands over his/her head and pretend that he/she is a turtle in a warm cozy shell where he or she can relax. The child is told that when he/she feels calm again, he or she can put the hands down and come out of the shell. This is a self-management technique. In the beginning we will have to cue the child, but then the child will have to do the turtle technique without cueing. At the end of the day, you give the child stickers for each time during the day that the turtle technique was used.

Some children relax more quickly if you cue them to take deep, slow breaths while they are in their turtle shell.

Mini-Program 4: **Teaching a Child to Stop**

In order to teach a child to stop, first run the "come here" drill below: Stand the child up with his/her back against the wall. Hold him or her by his/her shirt and say the child's name followed by, "come here." Gently pull the child to you. When the child gets to you, praise the child and hug him or her. Then gently push the child back against the wall and repeat 10 times. Try to use less and less force as you pull the child to you. If the child will come without pulling him or her to you, great, but always make the child come to you. Give the child a short break after the 10 trials and then repeat the drill.

An alternative way to run this drill requires two people. Get several feet apart. One person says the child's name followed by "come here." The other person holding the child gently pushes the child toward the person giving the command. As soon as the child gets there, praise the child and turn him or her around. Then the other person gives the command and the child is gently pushed toward the person who is now giving the command. As soon as the child becomes compliant, gradually increase the distance.

Both of these procedures are errorless. In other words, the child is always made to comply. Fifty times a day is a good practice target for the "come here" drill.

After the child has learned to come to you when called, then introduce the "stop" drill command. As the child is coming toward you, hold up your hand and say, "stop." Praise the child for doing so. Once the child has learned to stop when he/she is coming toward you, then introduce the stop command when the child is going away from you. When the child is going away from you toward the other person say, "stop." If the child does so, praise the child. If the child does not stop, then the person the child is moving toward should hold up his or her hand to cue the child to stop. Repeat until the child stops every time and then have the person stop holding up his or her hand. Move outside to treat the child.

Mini-Program 5: **Teach a Child to Hurry Up**

Many children do not follow directions in a timely manner. They are easily distracted by the physical and social environment, lost in their thoughts, have difficulty processing auditory information, etc. In this drill we are going to speed up direction following.

1. Be sure that you are not giving directions more than one time. The program I gave you for following directions said, "only give the direction one time. If the child immediately follows the direction, then reinforce the child. If not, then it's time out."
2. Take the child into his or her room and let him/her play with a toy, watch a video, etc, anything the child enjoys. Ask the child to come to you and perform some simple task. (Follow the rules for giving directions.) As soon as you ask the child, set an egg timer for _____ seconds. If the child gets there in time, then reinforce the child. Tell the child that you appreciate him or her coming quickly. If the child takes too much time and does not make it before the timer goes off, then it is time out.
3. Once the child is performing, carry the timer with you at all times and set the timer every time you give a direction. Follow the procedure in No. 2 above.
4. After the child is "hurrying" to follow directions, fade the timer.

Images

Cover Image provided by Amazon.com, 2014

The following images were used under license from Shutterstock.com:

- Chapter 1 Section 1 Image Copyright Cheryl Casey, 2012
- Chapter 1 Section 2 Image Copyright Sweet Lana, 2012
- Chapter 1 Section 3 Image Copyright Frederick R. Matzen, 2012
- Chapter 2 Section 1 Image Copyright Rido, 2012
- Chapter 2 Section 2 Image Copyright Serhiy Kobyakov, 2012
- Chapter 2 Section 3 Image Copyright Darren Brode, 2012
- Chapter 2 Section 4 Image Copyright Refat, 2012
- Chapter 2 Section 5 Image Copyright auremar, 2012
- Chapter 2 Section 6 Image Copyright CandyBox Images, 2012
- Chapter 2 Section 7 Image Copyright OLJ Studio, 2012
- Chapter 2 Section 8 Image Copyright 3445128471, 2012
- Chapter 2 Section 9 Image Copyright jamiehooper, 2012
- Chapter 2 Section 11 Image Copyright DenisNata, 2012
- Chapter 2 Section 12 Image Copyright Anatema, 2012
- Chapter 2 Section 13 Image Copyright Zdorov Kirill Vladimirovich, 2012
- Chapter 2 Section 14 Image Copyright Ilike, 2012
- Chapter 2 Section 15 Image Copyright Suzanne Tucker, 2012
- Chapter 2 Section 16 Image Copyright Suzanne Tucker, 2012
- Chapter 2 Section 17 Image Copyright Irina Magrelo, 2012
- Chapter 2 Section 18 Image Copyright Zurijeta, 2012
- Chapter 2 Section 19 Image Copyright Eric Isselée, 2012
- Chapter 2 Section 20 Image Copyright Blaj Gabriel, 2012
- Chapter 2 Section 21 Image Copyright Zurijeta, 2012
- Chapter 2 Section 22 Image Copyright oliveromg, 2012
- Chapter 2 Section 23 Image Copyright auremar, 2012
- Chapter 2 Section 24 Image Copyright olly, 2012
- Chapter 2 Section 25 Image Copyright ZouZou, 2012
- Chapter 3 Section 1 Image Copyright Darren Baker, 2012
- Chapter 3 Section 2 Image Copyright swissmacky, 2012
- Chapter 3 Section 3 Image Copyright Leah-Anne Thompson, 2012
- Chapter 3 Section 4 Image Copyright KellyBoreson, 2012
- Chapter 3 Section 5 Image Copyright Markus Gann, 201

ABOUT THE AUTHOR

Dr. Brown received his undergraduate degree from Texas Christian University in 1966 and stayed on as a Research Fellow in Medical Psychology receiving his Ph. D. in 1970. He spent 38 years at The University of Tennessee at Martin, 24 as Chair of the Psychology Department where he published over 30 journal articles, and several books and eBooks. He has maintained a private practice since 1970. In 2007 he retired from the university and founded The Children's Treatment Center (http: Childrenstreatmentcenter4autism.com) because the "autism epidemic" had expanded his practice and required his full time.

Dr. Brown still maintains a research program exploring the etiology (causes) of autism and a website ABA4Autism.com. Dr. Brown is a member of the Tennessee Psychological Association, Psi Chi, Sigma Xi, and the American Association for the Advancement of Science. Dr. Brown has been married for 48 years to his wife Carolyn who is practice manager. They have 2 daughters and 4 grandchildren.

Made in the USA
San Bernardino, CA
23 July 2015